"A wonderf good news tour of the message of the entire New Testament. In short, an excellent introductory book on the message of the New Testament."

Tom Schreiner, Professor of New Testament Interpretation and Professor of Biblical Theology, Southern Baptist Theological Seminary

"A concise and practical Christ-centered history of the New Testament that does not miss the forest for the trees. This book illuminates the New Testament by guiding the reader through key events and explaining their theological significance, helping the reader see how all the pieces fit together."

Brandon Crowe, Professor of New Testament at Westminster Theological Seminary

"Mitch Chase has produced an exciting book that will enthuse you for the Bible and make you wonder at God's amazing plan of salvation. A great tool to help Christians grow in their understanding of how the whole Bible story fits together and points to Jesus."

Alistair Chalmers, author of *Road Map to Jesus*

GOOD NEWS

FOR ALL THE EARTH

UNDERSTANDING
THE STORY OF
THE NEW TESTAMENT

GOOD NEWS

FOR ALL THE EARTH

MITCHELL L. CHASE

First published in Great Britain in 2025

British Library Cataloguing in Publication Data
A record for this book is available from the British Library

ISBN: 978-1-83728-032-2

Designed by Pete Barnsley (CreativeHoot.com)

Printed in UK

10Publishing, a division of 10ofthose.com
Unit C, Tomlinson Road, Leyland, PR25 2DY, England

Email: info@10ofthose.com
Website: www.10ofthose.com

1 3 5 7 10 8 6 4 2

For mom and dad.

May you always
believe, love, and sing
the good news.

CONTENTS

A SELECT TIMELINE

The following list of dates is a timeline of major events right before and during the New Testament period.

331 BC	Greece conquered Persia
146 BC	Rome conquered Greece
37–4 BC	Herod the Great was king of Judea
27 BC – AD 14	Augustus reigned as emperor of Rome
6–4 BC	The window of time for John the Baptist's birth
6–4 BC	The window of time for Jesus' birth
AD 14–37	Tiberius reigned as emperor of Rome

AD 26–37	Pilate was governor of Judea
AD 28 or 29	The time when John the Baptist's ministry began
AD 29 or 30	The time when Jesus' earthly ministry began
AD 33	The death, resurrection, and ascension of Jesus
AD 33–62	The years covered in the book of Acts
AD 33 or 34	The likely conversion of Paul
AD 40s to 60s	Paul's missionary journeys and letter writing
AD 66 or 67	The martyrdom of Paul in Rome
AD 70	The destruction of the Jerusalem temple

INTRODUCTION:

THE NEW COVENANT CHRONICLES

During the first-century Roman Empire, an explosion of literature told the riveting account of a man from Nazareth and the people who followed him. This collection of work is called the New Testament, and its documents were all written in approximately fifty years.

If such a scope and flurry of writing took place in such a short amount of time, people must have believed something important had happened. The New Testament authors believed they were writing the continuation of an older story that was left unfinished for centuries. This older story is the one the Old Testament tells. It's the story of God's plan to save the world through a promised son.

The Old Testament storyline takes us from creation to the 400s BC. The canvas is vast, covering multiple millennia, many empires, and various regions in the ancient Near East.

By contrast, the New Testament story starts small. It focuses on the land of Israel and a person named Jesus. Other names appear along the way, but he is the main character. The fourfold account of Jesus is found in the Gospels of Matthew, Mark, Luke, and John. These are the four books at the head of the New Testament. They tell of Jesus' birth, life, ministry, death, resurrection, and ascension.

After the four Gospels is the book of Acts. This book is a selective history of the first thirty years of the early church. Acts narrates the geographical expansion of the message about Jesus, moving from Jerusalem to Judea to Samaria to the end of the earth. We read about suffering and perseverance. We hear speeches and trials. We see conversions and miracles. In Acts, the risen and ascended Jesus is building his church.

The next block of New Testament literature consists of letters (or epistles). From Romans to Jude, there are twenty-one letters written by various authors to various recipients. The letters' authors aim to encourage, correct, admonish, teach, update, and warn the recipients about all manner of things. The volume of epistles is a testimony to their importance for Christian discipleship. The writers interpret how the Old Testament points to Jesus, ground the readers in doctrinal truths, and apply wisdom for Christian living.

At the end of the New Testament is the book of Revelation, sometimes called the Apocalypse. It is the capstone of the whole Bible, pulling the threads of the biblical story together in a glorious consummation. Addressed to several churches, the book of Revelation encourages their faithfulness and reminds them of God's promises. The wicked would be judged, and the righteous would be delivered. A future resurrection would defeat death, and all things would become new.

The Old Testament promises and prophecies find fulfillment in the person and work of Jesus Christ. The New Testament story tells of the dawn of hope, with the arrival of the grace and mercy of God in his beloved Son. Light has come into the world, and we need to understand what that means. What did Jesus come to do? How did his ministry connect to Old Testament expectations? What did his teachings and deeds reveal about his identity? How did the biblical authors relate the work of Christ to the lives of his disciples? And why should you care about any of this?

In order to answer these questions and more, we will proceed through eight chapters that overview the story of the New Testament. Chapter 1 takes us into the story of Christ's birth and the surrounding events. Chapter 2 transports us to the wilderness where Jesus faced temptation, and then we go to the Jordan River where he was baptized. Chapter 3 focuses on the teachings and miracles of Jesus. Chapter 4 surveys the events of Jesus' suffering and death. Chapter 5 celebrates the news of his resurrection and ascension. Chapter 6 is about the book of Acts, where the early church multiplies, and proclaims the gospel, and suffers for its message. Chapter 7 considers the purpose and themes of the New Testament letters. Chapter 8 closes our study by lifting our gaze to the hope that is to come—a hope found in the book of Revelation.

The many documents written about Jesus and his church in the first century are worthy of our patient attention and lifelong study. The twenty-seven books of the New Testament chronicle the new covenant—both the Christ who brought it and the community abiding in it. These chronicles are gospel—*good news*. This good news for all the earth is that a Savior has come, Jesus is his name, and whoever trusts in him will have everlasting life.

1

GOOD NEWS OF GREAT JOY

The Old Testament era had come to an end. Though our Bibles seem to move smoothly from Malachi to Matthew, the transition was not so quick. After the days of Malachi, four hundred years passed without a new word from God. But the lack of a prophet didn't mean the centuries were uneventful. The Old Testament era closed with Persia ruling over the promised land. But Persia eventually fell to Greece, and Greece to Rome.

As these nations fell and rose, the promised Messiah had not yet come. The promised kingdom had not been established. The offering of sacrifices continued at the temple in Jerusalem. Long lay the world in sin and error, pining and groaning for redemption.

Then, after centuries without a new word from the Lord, an angelic declaration broke the silence.

PREPARING THE WAY

A priest named Zechariah was in the temple to offer incense when he encountered an angel of the Lord. This was no normal day in the temple. In the Old Testament, an angel's appearance was a sign of something important underway. What news did this heavenly being bring?

Zechariah would have a son with his barren wife Elizabeth (Luke 1:13). This conception, like those of barren women in the Old Testament, was miraculous. The power of God would enable Elizabeth to conceive. And her son, John, would be the forerunner of the Messiah.

This John was the "Elijah" promised in Malachi 4:5: "Behold, I will send you Elijah the prophet before the great and awesome day of the Lord comes." The future Elijah would prepare the way for the Lord. Malachi's words confirm that John's role connected to ancient expectations that had remained unfulfilled for centuries.

The reference to Elizabeth's barrenness (Luke 1:7) was part of an earlier pattern in the Old Testament, where a woman's barrenness was mentioned in order for the biblical author to narrate its reversal. Just as Sarah, Rebekah, Rachel, Manoah's wife, and Hannah all conceived because of God's power upon their womb, so also Elizabeth would be with child. Though the Old Testament authors reported a handful of barren women who gave birth, John's mother Elizabeth is the only such woman mentioned in the New Testament.

The angelic announcement of a child to a barren woman would be good news for the family, but the news had impact elsewhere too. John's birth was good news not because he was the Savior, but because he would testify about the Savior. As the fourth Gospel tells us, "There was a man sent from God, whose name was John. He came as a witness, to bear witness about the light, that all might believe through him. He was not the light, but came to bear witness about the light" (John 1:6–8).

If John's mission was to bear witness about the world's saving Light, then his generation would be the generation to see the long-awaited Christ. When we read about John's birth, we can marvel at the promise-keeping character of God. Divine promises require patience, but the waiting is never in vain. John was born because God is trustworthy. And John was born from a woman who had been barren because a miraculous conception drew attention to divine power.

A VIRGIN NAMED MARY

The miraculous conceptions in the Old Testament were surpassed by what God did in the life of a young virgin named Mary. The angel Gabriel appeared to this girl in Nazareth of Galilee, and he said, "Do not be afraid, Mary, for you have found favor with God. And behold, you will conceive in your womb and bear a son, and you shall call his name Jesus" (Luke 1:30–31).

This promised son of Mary was the long-awaited son from Eve, the seed of the woman who would defeat the serpent (Gen. 3:15). Mary's son would also be the prophesied son of David (2 Sam. 7:12–13). The angel told her, "He will be great and will be called the Son of the Most High. And the Lord God will give to him the throne of his father David, and he will reign over the house of Jacob forever, and of his kingdom there will be no end" (Luke 1:32–33).

Mary's son would be the Christ, the king from David's line, the one from Judah's tribe who would hold the scepter forever (Gen. 49:10). The predicament for Mary, however, was her unmarried state. "How will this be," she asked, "since I am a virgin?" (Luke 1:34). Mary knew, as everyone did in the ancient world, that conception requires a man and woman.

The angel's answer was stunning: "The Holy Spirit will come upon you, and the power of the Most High will overshadow you; therefore the child to be born will be called holy—the Son of God" (Luke 1:35). The overshadowing Spirit recalls Genesis 1, where the Spirit hovered over the waters (Gen. 1:2). The Creator would say "Let there be life" to Mary's womb. When people refer to the miracle of the virgin birth, what they are referring to is the virginal *conception*. The reason the virgin Mary gave birth was because of the miraculous conception in her womb.

Because of the Holy Spirit's power upon Mary's womb, she would conceive a child, and the child would be holy, without sin. The human nature of Jesus was like Adam's before Adam and Eve rebelled against God; Jesus' human nature was uncorrupted though mortal. His sinless nature was not contingent on Mary's nature. She was a sinner while also being the one who bore the sinless Son of God in her womb.

In the words of John 1:14, "the Word became flesh and dwelt among us." The language of dwelling evokes the tabernacle which dwelt in the midst of Israel's camp in the Old Testament. The tabernacle—and later the temple—signaled God's presence with his people. The tabernacling of God's Son is called the *incarnation*, the enfleshment of—or the taking of a human nature by—the person of the Son. With language that staggers the imagination, we can say that the Son of God is truly divine and truly man. Jesus was right when he said, "something greater than the temple is here" (Matt. 12:6).

DAVID'S SON IN DAVID'S TOWN

In the days of Caesar Augustus, a royal decree called for the people to register in their hometowns, so Joseph and Mary made plans to travel to Bethlehem (Luke 2:1–5).

The journey from Nazareth to Bethlehem was approximately eighty miles and would take several days, perhaps as much as a week because Mary was pregnant.

Why do the biblical authors draw attention to Bethlehem? Because Micah prophesied that the future ruler over Israel would come from Bethlehem (Mic. 5:2). Through the decree about the people registering in their hometowns, Mary ended up in the right place for the birth of Jesus. The sovereignty of the Lord ensured that Micah's prophecy was fulfilled.

Bethlehem's significance precedes Micah's prophecy. King David was born in Bethlehem. When the time had come for a new king to be identified who would replace Saul, Samuel went to Bethlehem and to the house of Jesse (1 Sam. 16). The Lord told Samuel, "I will send you to Jesse the Bethlehemite, for I have provided for myself a king among his sons" (1 Sam. 16:1).

After examining Jesse's sons, Samuel discerns that David shall be the future king, and Samuel anoints him (1 Sam. 16:6–14). This Bethlehemite would be king, and one day his Descendant from Bethlehem would be king too.

The little town of Bethlehem was unimportant from a worldly perspective. It was not a place for the social and political elites. It was not a hotspot of commercial and economic momentum. Bethlehem would have had several hundred residents in the days of Jesus, an unimpressive number of people inhabiting an unimpressive place.

But God's ways are not our ways. He subverted the wisdom of the world by confounding the criteria of importance. From tiny Bethlehem would come the promised ruler. There, in David's hometown, David's greater Son would be born to reign.

A HOUSE AND A MANGER

Mary and Joseph rushed around Bethlehem trying to find a place for Mary to give birth, and since the innkeeper refused to give them any space in the inn, she was forced to have the baby in a nearby stable. Isn't that how the story goes? Isn't that what happened?

Even though it's a popular retelling of the events, that's not what happened. Speaking about the couple in Bethlehem, the writer says, "And while they were there, the time came for her to give birth" (Luke 2:6). This verse suggests that they were already staying in Bethlehem when Mary's labor began.

But where were Mary and Joseph staying? While a popular notion is that an innkeeper had denied them a room, that, too, is not exactly what the text tells us. Since Joseph had a family history in Bethlehem, he would have done what others traveling back to Bethlehem would have done: stayed with relatives.

We should imagine Mary and Joseph staying with members of Joseph's family—in a *house*. We learn from Luke 2:7 that "there was no place for them in the inn," but that word "inn" has caused confusion. The term is not what you would expect to read if an inn or motel was in view. It is the word for "guest room." An inn would be where guests stay, but an Israelite home could have a guest room as well.

Luke 2:7 is telling us that there was no place for Mary to give birth in the guest room of the house. This situation was probably due to others, besides Mary and Joseph, staying in the house with Joseph's relatives.

After Mary gave birth to Jesus, she swaddled him and laid him in a manger (Luke 2:7). A manger refers to the place where animal owners placed feed and straw. The humble circumstances of the promised son are surprising. He is born not in a major city accompanied by fanfare; he is born in Bethlehem, a small village in Galilee. He does not lie upon a regal and expensive bed; Mary places the newborn king in a feeding trough.

SHEPHERDS KEEPING WATCH

In the same region of Bethlehem, shepherds were watching their flocks at night. An angel suddenly appeared to them and said, "Fear not, for behold, I bring you good news of great joy that will be for all the people. For unto you is born this day in the city of David a Savior, who is Christ the Lord" (Luke 2:10–11).

The good news was a Savior's birth, and this Savior was the promised king. The angel's words allude to Isaiah 9:6–7, where we read about the birth of a son who would be the Christ and would reign on David's throne.

Marvel at the wisdom of God in revealing this good news to shepherds in a field. This news did not come first to the socially connected or the religiously astute. Lowly shepherds in the region of Bethlehem were the first to hear about the Messiah's birth. The angel even told them of the humble circumstances they would find: "And this will be a sign for you: you will find a baby wrapped in swaddling cloths and lying in a manger" (Luke 2:12).

The shepherds left to find the Christ child, and they went "with haste" (Luke 2:16). Coming to the house, they saw the child as the angel had foretold, and "they made known the saying that had been told them concerning this child" (2:17). This confirmation was especially important to Mary, who "treasured up all these things, pondering them in her heart" (2:19). The angel Gabriel had previously told her that the child would be the promised king from David's line (1:32–33), and now shepherds have learned this same truth (2:11).

Imagine this small group of witnesses. These shepherds are beholding Israel's great Shepherd, the one whose voice will call sinners to himself and who will lay his life down for his sheep.

GIFTS FROM THE EAST

At some point after Jesus' birth, wise men from the east came to find him and bring him gifts. Because Herod the Great sought to kill children in Bethlehem who were two years old or under (Matt. 2:16), the span of time between Jesus' birth and the wise men's visit would've been less than two years.

These Gentiles from the east are reminiscent of Old Testament expectations that people from the nations would seek the Lord (see, for example, Isa. 2:1–5). In Israel's history, "the east" had been the place of Babylonian exile. God exiled the Israelites to Babylon for a period of seventy years, and then the exiles returned from the east to the promised land (2 Chron. 36; Ezra 1–2).

The arrival of these magi in Matthew 2 also reminds us of Solomon's visit from the queen of Sheba. The queen had heard of Solomon's fame, and she came to him with gifts—including gold and spices (1 Kgs. 10:1–2, 10). Note, then, that a Gentile from another land brought gifts to Solomon, the son of David. Matthew 2:1–12 is about Gentiles from another land bringing gifts to the Son of David, the promised Savior.

The magi arrived at "the house" and saw Mary with Jesus (Matt. 2:11). This house was likely the same location where Mary and Joseph stayed upon arriving in Bethlehem (Luke 2:1–7).

The Gentile travelers presented gifts of gold, frankincense, and myrrh (Matt. 2:11). These were not normal gifts to mark the birth of a baby. But they were gifts fit for a king. And a king was exactly who the magi believed the newborn baby to be (Matt. 2:2).

After their visit with the child and his family, the magi received a warning in a dream not to return to Herod, so they went home by a different route (Matt. 2:12). Joseph, too, had a dream with a warning. Herod planned to search for the child and destroy him, so Joseph took Mary and Jesus and left for Egypt (2:13–14).

Ironically, the place of Israel's former captivity had become a place of refuge for the Son of God. Herod's murderous plans for the babies of Bethlehem recalls the beginning of the book of Exodus, where Pharaoh ordered the killing of all the Israelite baby boys (Exod. 1:15–16).

In Exodus 2, Moses was spared from the murderous plans of Pharaoh. He was born to deliver his people. In Matthew 2, Jesus was spared from the murderous plans of Herod. He, too, was born to deliver his people. He would be even greater than Moses. He would "save his people from their sins" (Matt. 1:21).

WISDOM AND STATURE

As you would expect from a human, Jesus developed and aged. Luke tells us, "And the child grew and became strong, filled with wisdom. And the favor of God was upon him" (Luke 2:40). Furthermore, "Jesus increased in wisdom and in stature and in favor with God and man" (2:52).

The Lord Jesus is one person with two natures. When Luke writes about Jesus growing in wisdom and stature, that is a reference to the humanity of Christ. The doctrine of Christology (which is the Bible's teaching about the person and work of Christ) takes us into deep waters. Nevertheless, if the biblical authors teach that Jesus has genuine deity and genuine humanity, then we must learn to speak of Christ's person and work without denying to him the characteristics of either nature.

According to Luke's Gospel, Jesus grows in wisdom. He is truly human, with a human body and mind and will. Even as a child, Jesus conducted himself with reverence and never with sin. In the only scene Luke gives us of Jesus as a young man, Jesus is in the Jerusalem temple listening, asking questions, and giving answers (Luke 2:46).

But Jerusalem was not where Jesus lived. He grew up in Nazareth (Matt. 2:23; Luke 2:39), where he would have attended the local synagogue and learned the words of God. Part of Jesus' growth in wisdom would have involved the embrace of and submission to what Scripture taught. He would internalize the words of the Old Testament upon his heart. His own words and actions would be shaped by what was true, good, honorable, and wise.

Year by year, the days drew nearer to the time when a wild voice in the wilderness would cry out, "Prepare the way of the Lord!"

UNDERSTANDING JESUS

- The births of John the Baptist and Jesus were both prophesied by angels and accomplished by divine power.
- The Son of God took to himself a truly human nature without changing or negating his divine nature.

- The name "Jesus" is connected to his mission, because it means "Yahweh is salvation."
- The humble circumstances of Jesus' birth highlight the wisdom of God that confounds the ways of the world.

SUGGESTED READING

- Exodus 1:8 – 2:10
- 2 Samuel 7:1–17
- Matthew 2:16–23
- John 1:1–18

2

FROM THE RIVER TO THE WILDERNESS

The boy Jesus became a man, growing in wisdom and stature into his adulthood. Before inaugurating his public ministry, Jesus was baptized by John the Baptist in the Jordan River and tempted by the devil in the wilderness.

Reflecting on Jesus' baptism helps us think about his identity, and understanding the scenes of temptation helps us affirm his sinlessness. His baptism and temptations also connect us to the Old Testament, where background from Adam and Israel illuminates these episodes that lead to Jesus' public ministry.

THE BAPTIZER

Zechariah's son, John, was the forerunner of the Messiah and a prophet in the wilderness. He called people to repent and proclaimed to them a baptism of repentance (Matt. 3:2; Luke 3:3). His voice in the wilderness was the fulfillment of earlier prophecy. Isaiah 40 spoke of a voice crying in the wilderness, "Prepare the way of the Lord" (Isa. 40:3; Luke 3:4). And John was this voice.

John's acts of baptism weren't done in Jerusalem. He was immersing people in the Jordan River. In fact, "all the country of Judea and all Jerusalem were going out to him and were being baptized by him in the river Jordan, confessing their sins" (Mark 1:5).

The Jordan River recalls the Old Testament book of Joshua, which narrates the Israelites' conquest of the promised land. Like they did at the Red Sea to escape Pharoah, the Israelites crossed the Jordan River on dry ground to receive their inheritance (Josh. 3:16–17). Once again, the Jordan River was important in the biblical narrative. According to the Gospels, people were baptized by John in this body of water.

After centuries without a prophet from God, here was a voice in the wilderness. John was even dressed like a prophet—a *specific* prophet. He wore a garment of camel's hair and a leather belt around his waist (Matt. 3:4), and this style evoked the prophet Elijah. According to 2 Kings 1:8, Elijah wore a garment of hair and a belt of leather around his waist.

The description of John in the Gospels is meant to connect him to Elijah. The reason for this connection is the prophecy in Malachi 4. God promised to send "Elijah the prophet" before the Messiah came (Mal. 4:5; see also 3:1). And Jesus identified John the Baptist as the "Elijah who is to come" (Matt. 11:14).

The Old Testament resonances in John's life were external clues to his significance—the significance both of his message and of his baptisms in the Jordan River.

THE BAPTISM OF JESUS

Since John proclaimed a baptism of repentance, and since people responded to his call by confessing their sins (Matt. 3:5–6), we need to reflect on why Jesus came to John for baptism. Has that event ever seemed strange to you? It certainly seemed strange to John, who said to Jesus, "I need to be baptized by you, and do you come to me?" (Matt. 3:14).

Jesus had no sins to confess, so there was no need to repent. Nevertheless, Jesus traveled more than sixty miles from Galilee to the Jordan River to be baptized by John (Matt. 3:13). If Jesus wasn't a repentant sinner getting baptized, then the deliberate immersion into the Jordan River meant something else.

Though not a sinner himself, Jesus came to identify with sinners. His baptism was an example he wanted others to follow. After his resurrection, he commanded his disciples to baptize disciples (Matt. 28:19–20). Baptism was a picture of death and new life. When believers in Christ are baptized, the act pictures their death to sin and the new life they possess through union with Christ (Rom. 6:1–4).

In the Old Testament, the Israelites were a people who went through the waters. They went through the Red Sea, an event that Paul described as being "baptized into Moses in the cloud and in the sea" (1 Cor. 10:2). And they went through the waters of the Jordan River as they entered the promised land. These events are the background to Jesus' own baptism. He is a true and better Israel. According to Exodus 4:22, Israel was God's son, and they came through the waters. In the Gospels, Jesus is God's Son who goes through the waters.

When Jesus emerged from the waters, the Spirit descended upon him like a dove (Matt. 3:16), and the Father said, "This is my beloved Son, with whom I am well pleased" (3:17). This scene signals that Jesus is the Servant from the prophecies of Isaiah. In Isaiah 42:1, the Lord says through the prophet, "Behold my servant, whom I uphold, my chosen, in whom my soul delights; I have put my Spirit upon him; he will bring forth justice to the nations." The Spirit's descent upon Christ identifies him as the chosen servant of the Lord. God's delight in the servant is echoed in the Father's words ("with whom I am well pleased").

The voice at Christ's baptism also called him "my beloved Son," which alludes to Genesis 22:2 (when God told Abraham, "Take your son, your only son Isaac, whom you love") and Psalm 2:7 (where God said to the promised king, "You are my Son; today I have begotten you").

One of the ways to understand the baptism of Jesus is as an anointing. This signifies his kingship. Jesus is the Messiah, the Anointed One, the *King*. The Spirit descends upon him, the Father confirms his identity, and the Son emerges from the waters of the Jordan ready to lead the new exodus he was born to accomplish.

But first, the true Israel must go into the wilderness.

LED INTO THE WILDERNESS

The fourth chapter of Matthew's Gospel opens with a line that is both blunt and startling: "Then Jesus was led up by the Spirit into the wilderness to be tempted by the devil" (Matt. 4:1).

Jesus faced temptation so that he would be faithful, whereas Israel before him, and Adam before them, failed and were unfaithful. The Spirit led Jesus into the wilderness, and Jesus faced the devil after forty days of fasting (Matt. 4:2–3). The Son was prepared for the adversary.

A narrated personal encounter between the tempter and his prey is something we read at both the beginning of the Old Testament and the beginning of the New Testament. Adam and Eve encountered the tempter in Genesis 3, and they sinned. They disbelieved God's true words and trusted Satan's twisted words instead.

Now a new Adam would confront the devil. But this region in Matthew 4 was no garden of Eden. This was a *wilderness*, which was reminiscent of Israel's journey between Egypt and the promised land. Between their deliverance and receiving their inheritance, the Israelites traveled through the wilderness. And the wilderness was a place of their temptation, the place where they failed to trust God (see, for example, the stories in Exod. 15:22–27; 16:1–8; 17:1–7; Num. 11:1–15; 12:1–9; 13:25 – 14:12).

Because of their disobedience in Numbers 13–14, the Israelites wandered in the wilderness for forty years before Joshua led a new generation into the promised land (Num. 14:26–38). A period of "forty" corresponds to Jesus' temptations in Matthew 4. He was in the wilderness for forty days (Matt. 4:2). Jesus was a new Adam and the true Israel. He would be the obedient Son. Led by the Spirit into the wilderness, the Son would trust the Father. And he would subdue the devil.

THE FIRST TEMPTATION

The serpent came to the seed of the woman with a test: "If you are the Son of God, command these stones to become loaves of bread" (Matt. 4:3). Of course, the Lord Jesus could have commanded these stones to do just that—to become bread for the Son of God. This would have been just as the rock in the wilderness broke forth with water for the Israelites (see Exod. 17:1–7).

But the goal of Jesus' miraculous power was not to serve his own interests. The Son had been fasting for forty days, and he needed no prompting from the evil one to seek food. The devil draws attention to Jesus' sonship ("If you are the Son of God") to portray the Son as being unhelped, uncared for. Though Jesus is God's Son, he is nevertheless hungry. Jesus, so the tempter suggested, needed to provide for himself because he apparently couldn't depend on his Father.

Jesus responded to this first temptation by quoting Deuteronomy: "It is written, 'Man shall not live by bread alone, but by every word that comes from the mouth of God'" (Matt. 4:4, quoting Deut. 8:3). This quotation from Deuteronomy is significant when we recall the context of Moses' words to the Israelites.

Before Moses spoke the line which Jesus quoted, he had told the people,

> *And you shall remember the whole way that the LORD your God has led you these forty years in the wilderness, that he might humble you, testing you to know what was in your heart, whether you would keep his commandments or not. And he humbled you and let you hunger and fed you with manna, which you did not know, nor did your fathers know, that he might make you know that man does not live by bread alone, but man lives by every word that comes from the mouth of the LORD (Deut. 8:2–3).*

The Israelites failed to trust God. But the Son would not fail. If Israel's tests revealed what was in their heart, so also would Jesus' testing in the wilderness reveal what was in his heart—a delight in God's word, an unwavering trust in his Father, and a discerning eye that exposed Satan's attempts to deceive him.

Jesus' quote from Deuteronomy 8:3 asserted that the spiritual sustenance of God's word mattered more than the physical sustenance of bread. God's word was a better, more lasting bread.

THE SECOND TEMPTATION

A second temptation took place. The devil took Jesus to Jerusalem and set him on the pinnacle of the temple (Matt. 4:5). Are we to imagine an actual and sudden physical relocation for this temptation? Perhaps Matthew is reporting some kind of visionary experience.

With Jesus atop the temple, the devil says, "If you are the Son of God, throw yourself down, for it is written, 'He will command his angels concerning you,' and, 'On their hands they will bear you up, lest you strike your foot against a stone'" (Matt. 4:6). The devil was quoting Psalm 91:11–12. His challenge was for Jesus to publicly display his messianic identity in a flashy, showman-like way.

But such an ostentatious act was not the purpose of Jesus' identity and work. He came to serve, to humble himself, to lay down his life. Jesus told the devil, "Again it is written, 'You shall not put the Lord your God to the test'" (Matt. 4:7, quoting Deut. 6:16). If Jesus followed the devil's guidance, he would be putting God to the test.

Even though the devil quoted Scripture in the temptation, he used the psalm incorrectly. Psalm 91:11–12 was not about putting the Lord to the test by throwing oneself from a high elevation in order to be caught by angels. Just as the devil did in Genesis 3, he took God's good words and twisted them.

Jesus' response was a quotation of Deuteronomy 6:16. Moses had told the Israelites, "You shall not put the LORD your God to the test, as you tested him at Massah" (Deut. 6:16). The Israelites had tested the Lord in the wilderness (see Exod. 17:1–7), and now the devil was tempting Jesus to test the Lord in the wilderness. Jesus refused to play the devil's game.

Psalm 91:11–12 wasn't an untrue passage; the devil simply misapplied it. The verses in that psalm were meant to encourage the reader to trust the Lord's delivering hand and the hands of his delivering angels. However, the devil wielded those words for a different purpose. Furthermore, he didn't include verse 13 in his tempting words, a verse which says, "You will tread on the lion and the adder; the young lion and the serpent you will trample underfoot." How convenient that the devil stopped quoting where he did, right before the image of a foot crushing a serpent.

THE THIRD TEMPTATION

For the third temptation, the devil took Jesus to a very high mountain (Matt. 4:8). The temptations get higher and higher. The first was apparently on the ground of the wilderness. The second was on the pinnacle of the Jerusalem temple. And the third is on a high mountain.

From this vantage point, Satan "showed him all the kingdoms of the world and their glory. And he said to him, 'All these I will give you, if you will fall down and worship me'" (Matt. 4:8–9). For the third time, Jesus quoted Deuteronomy. He said, "Be gone, Satan! For it is written, 'You shall worship the Lord your God and him only shall you serve'" (Matt. 4:10, quoting Deut. 6:13).

A bit more context for Jesus' quote is found in these additional words from Deuteronomy:

> *. . . then take care lest you forget the* Lord, *who brought you out of the land of Egypt, out of the house of slavery. It is the* Lord *your God you shall fear. Him you shall serve and by his*

> *name you shall swear. You shall not go after other gods, the gods of the peoples who are around you (Deut. 6:12–14).*

Giving in to the devil's temptation would mean false worship, and the Son of God would never break the commands of God. Besides, Psalm 2 tells us what the Father promised the Son: "Ask of me, and I will make the nations your heritage, and the ends of the earth your possession. You shall break them with a rod of iron and dash them in pieces like a potter's vessel" (Ps. 2:8–9).

Jesus didn't need the twisted and deceptive words of the devil promising him the nations of the earth. He already had the sure and altogether trustworthy word of his Father.

DOMINION IN THE WILDERNESS

After the third temptation, Matthew tells us, "Then the devil left him, and behold, angels came and were ministering to him" (Matt. 4:11). The tempter had failed in his plans, and the Son stood victorious in the wilderness. He had resisted the devil's temptations and responded each time with the truth of Scripture.

Matthew 4 is about the true Israel, Jesus, trusting God's words and not testing the Lord. It is about the new Adam, Jesus, exercising dominion over the tempter and refusing to believe his twisted speech. The wilderness had been a place of failure in Exodus and Numbers, but in the Gospels it was a place of the long-awaited king's faithfulness.

Let us pause to ponder the fact that, before Jesus traveled to preach, before he healed the sick or raised the dead, before he spoke in parables or walked on water, he subdued the evil one. The devil, says the text, *left him*. Luke's Gospel clarifies that the devil would reconvene his deceptions at a future date: "he departed from him until an opportune time" (Luke 4:13).

No further opportune time between Jesus and the devil is narrated in the Gospels, but further traps would still await him. The religious leaders would embody the serpent's deceptive and malicious demeanor. In Matthew 22:15, for instance, "the Pharisees went and plotted how to entangle him in his words." Whether from Satan or Pharisees or Sadducees or scribes, no trap could ensnare him. Jesus would subdue their efforts and evade their snares. His dominion spread wherever he went.

We know what it's like to face temptations in this fallen world. We are vulnerable to our indwelling sins and to external snares. We may be tempted to doubt God's words, misuse Scripture, feel the allure of false worship, and wonder if God's commands and promises are for our good. The same devil tells the same lies.

As we read about Jesus' victory over sin and Satan in the wilderness, we can be encouraged by his faithfulness and blamelessness. We can exult in the unfailing obedience of God's Son. Though the first Adam sinned and we fell to spiritual death in him, the last Adam prevailed and in him we shall live.

UNDERSTANDING JESUS

- Jesus' baptism in the Jordan River recalled the importance of that river in the history of the Old Testament Israelites.
- The Father's voice at the Son's baptism identified the Son as the prophesied servant and king.

- As the Israelites were tempted in the wilderness, Jesus was tempted in the wilderness.
- Jesus' dominion over the evil one's temptations shows that Jesus is a new Adam who would be faithful in contrast to the first Adam who sinned.

SUGGESTED READING

- Genesis 3:1–7
- Numbers 13:1 – 14:38
- Romans 6:1–11
- Hebrews 3:1 – 4:16

3

KINGDOM WORDS AND WONDERS

When you read about the miracles and teachings of Jesus, where do you imagine him? Do you see him in a home? Do you see him teaching and healing those along the roadside? Do you see him in a specific town, like Nazareth? Do you see certain audiences, like the poor or like the religious leaders?

The ministry of Christ did not unfold in only one location. He traveled and preached, and this activity took place throughout the promised land. The four Gospels tell us about the kinds of things he preached, the parables he told, and the claims he made.

We also learn about kingdom signs and wonders, miracles which shine the light of hope that the Savior has come who will bring healing and transformation to both body and soul.

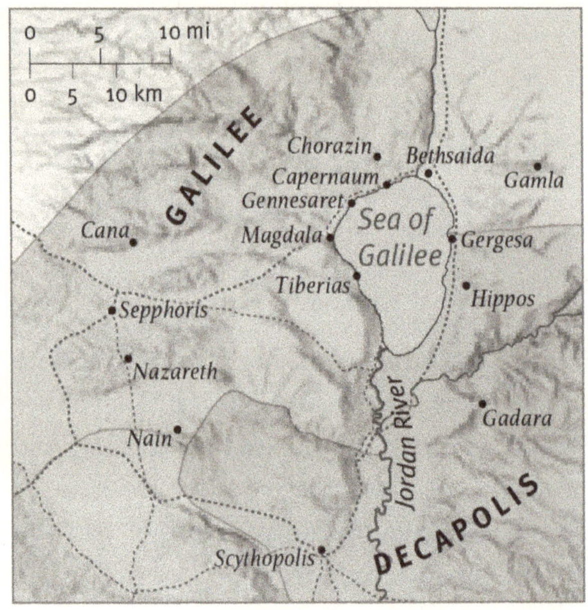

A DAWNING LIGHT

The region of Galilee was in the northern part of Israel, and Jesus stayed in the town of Capernaum, on the northern edge of the Sea of Galilee. According to Matthew's Gospel, this was the territory of the ancient tribal territories of Zebulun and Naphtali (Matt. 4:13).

His presence in this part of the land was a fulfillment of Scripture (Matt. 4:14). According to the prophet Isaiah, "The land of Zebulun and the land of Naphtali, the way of the sea, beyond the Jordan, Galilee of the Gentiles—the people dwelling in darkness have seen a great light, and for those dwelling in the region and shadow of death, on them a light has dawned" (Matt. 4:15–16, quoting Isa. 9:1–2).

Matthew's quotation of Isaiah 9 is significant because the prophet's passage was about the coming king. Even though only the first two verses of that chapter are cited, those opening verses would naturally evoke the fuller context of the whole chapter. The prophet said, "For to us a child is born, to us a son is given; and the government shall be upon his shoulder, and his name shall be called Wonderful Counselor, Mighty God, Everlasting Father, Prince of Peace" (Isa. 9:6).

The connection between the son's birth and the Davidic kingdom is confirmed in Isaiah 9:7: "Of the increase of his government and of peace there will be no end, on the throne of David and over his kingdom, to establish it and to uphold it with justice and with righteousness from this time forth and forevermore. The zeal of the Lord of hosts will do this."

When Jesus is dwelling in Galilee, his presence there fulfills the hopes of Isaiah 9. Because Jesus is the light, his time in Capernaum means the shining of light in a land of deep darkness (Isa. 9:1–2; Matt. 4:12–16). Wherever Jesus goes, the light goes. Wherever Jesus dwells, the light dwells.

The dawning light of Jesus' ministry is relevant for more than just the Jews. Though Israelites pervaded the promised land, Isaiah 9:1 mentions Galilee of the Gentiles, and so a hope for all the nations is in view. Jesus came with a message for the world.

THE KINGDOM OF HEAVEN

Jesus preached, "Repent, for the kingdom of heaven is at hand" (Matt. 4:17). John the Baptist had earlier proclaimed this message (3:2), and he was preparing the way for the Lord. The beginning of Christ's ministry involved the proclamation of a kingdom.

What kingdom was anticipated? The answer to that question takes us back to 2 Samuel 7:12–

13, to the time when David learned that his future offspring would receive an everlasting throne. The Israelites would be on the lookout for the son of David who would reign forever.

The unending Davidic kingdom wasn't like other regimes. The prophet Daniel described this kingdom with rock imagery: "As you looked, a stone was cut out by no human hand ... the stone that struck the image became a great mountain and filled the whole earth" (Dan. 2:34–35). The interpretation came later in Daniel's prophecy: "And in the days of those kings the God of heaven will set up a kingdom that shall never be destroyed, nor shall the kingdom be left to another people. It shall break in pieces all these kingdoms and bring them to an end, and it shall stand forever" (2:44).

If God establishes a kingdom, then its origin is not the result of the military efforts and political ambitions of man. The origin is *heavenly*. The God of heaven establishes a kingdom of heaven, and this kingdom is the promised Davidic reign of the Messiah.

When Jesus proclaims that the kingdom of heaven is at hand, he does not mean the kingdom has come in fullness but that he has inaugurated the kingdom. The background from Daniel about the rock that becomes a mountain is helpful here. Just as the rock was not yet the mountain, Jesus' announcement of the Davidic kingdom is about its beginning and not its fullness.

CALLING THE TWELVE

Through his incarnation and ministry, God's Son, the Davidic king, has come to proclaim the message of the kingdom and to call to himself a kingdom people. When Jesus summoned others to follow him, their whole lives changed. Jesus reoriented their lives around himself. Do you see the implications of this for your own life? When we follow Christ, our lives are oriented around him. His words and example shape us.

The goal of Christian living isn't about trying to fit Jesus into our lives. The goal is the reordering of our lives, from the inside out, around him—the cultivation of a Christ-centered life. The disciples in the four Gospels experienced the disorientation and reorientation of following Jesus. Their priorities became kingdom-focused, and this impacted their previous commitments.

An example of this is the encounter between Jesus and some fishermen. He saw Simon and Andrew casting a net into the sea, and he said, "Follow me, and I will make you fishers of men" (Matt. 4:18–19). They left their nets to follow him. Leaving their nets was not just a literal act. The nets represented their lives. With a play on words, Jesus told these fishermen that they would still be fishing—but for a greater kind of fish. They would be catching people.

As Jesus ministered, people gathered and grew in number. Word about Jesus spread, so interest in him grew elsewhere as well. His fame spread beyond the land of Israel and into Syria. Great crowds even came from the Decapolis, which was east of Galilee and across the Jordan River.

Among the many followers of Jesus that accumulated, twelve names are etched in the Gospels as the twelve disciples. These twelve were a special group with whom Jesus spent significant time, traveled long distances, and shared kingdom insights. Their names were Simon Peter, Andrew, James the son of Zebedee, John, Philip, Bartholomew, Thomas, Matthew, James the son of Alphaeus, Thaddaeus, Simon the Zealot, and Judas.

The significance of twelve disciples is that the number recalls the tribes of Israel in the Old Testament. Jacob had twelve sons, and these sons were the heads of their descendants that comprised twelve tribes. When Jesus gathers an intimate group of followers, he doesn't choose nine or fifteen. The choice of twelve men suggests that he is accomplishing the renewal of Israel.

The backgrounds of these twelve men were varied. Several were fishermen, one was a tax collector, one had been a zealot (part of a movement that was zealously opposed to the Roman Empire). Some shared the same name (like Simon or James). Some were siblings (like James and John, the sons of Zebedee). And each time the list of disciples appears in the Gospels, Judas' name is last. He is the one "who betrayed him" (Matt. 10:4; see also Mark 3:19; Luke 6:16). While none of the disciples were perfect, one among them would commit the outrageous act of betraying the Son of God at the appointed time.

Having called the twelve to himself, Jesus had much to tell them—and much to tell everyone else too.

TEACHING ALONG THE WAY

Jesus talked everywhere and with anybody. He engaged the religious leaders and the outcasts. He spoke to Jews and Gentiles. He ministered to men and women, the young and old, the rich and poor, the powerful and powerless. He cared for them all. This scope of his compassion and instruction is encouraging because we realize that we are not excluded from his interest or focus. No matter who we are, no matter where we've come from, no matter what we've done, we are the kind of person for whom Jesus has come.

Jesus ministered in various venues. According to the Gospel records, he taught inside places like synagogues or houses, and outside in fields or standing in boats. He spoke privately to his disciples, and he taught publicly to thousands. He addressed people in his hometown of Nazareth as well as those who lived outside the land of Israel.

As Jesus taught, he proclaimed the gospel of the kingdom of God (Mark 1:14–15). People developed opinions about his identity, and he asked his disciples poignantly about it: "Who do people say that I am?" (Mark 8:27). The list of possibilities included John the Baptist (who had earlier been beheaded), Elijah, or one of the prophets. These options, of course, were incorrect.

He then asked the disciples, "But who do you say that I am?" (Mark 8:29). They had spent more time with Jesus, heard more of his teachings, and had longer to reflect on all that had been happening among and around them. Peter represented the group when he said, "You are the Christ" (8:29).

Jesus did not reject Peter's answer, because he was indeed the Christ. But the disciples did not fully grasp what the Christ had come to do. After Peter's confession, Jesus began to teach about his future suffering, death, and resurrection. And he taught this by using the title "Son of Man."

In fact, "Son of Man" was the title Jesus used the most for himself. It recalled Daniel 7, where one like a son of man came on the clouds of heaven to the Ancient of Days and received dominion over all things (Dan. 7:13–14). Jesus taught that the Son of Man must suffer many things, face rejection by Jewish leaders, and then die—but on the third day the Son of Man would rise again (Mark 8:31).

Jesus taught about other things, such as prayer and love and marriage and judgment and forgiveness. He interpreted the Old Testament, alluding to characters and events and even prefacing statements with "It is written" when he was going to quote from it. As the Son of God, he understood the Old Testament perfectly, so we can trust whatever interpretation he has authoritatively given.

Perhaps the most famous teaching discourse of Jesus is the Sermon on the Mount, which is the phrase summarizing Matthew 5–7. It is in these chapters that Jesus expounds kingdom truths and kingdom ethics. He directs his disciples to a life of obedience that flows out of a heart that seeks the Lord.

The teachings of Jesus were always wise, never foolish. Something greater than Solomon was here (Matt. 12:42). He explained the way of wisdom, and the way is the path that conforms to his own words. In fact, the person who is wise will listen to Jesus' words and do them (7:24–25). The fool is the one who hears Jesus' words and does something else (7:26–27).

Jesus wasn't a typical orator, and he made claims that exceeded the credibility of a normal rabbi. He made pronouncements like, "You have heard it said, but I say unto you ..." He spoke with awareness of the gravity and authority that his words carried. By the time you finish reading the Sermon on the Mount, you get the clear impression that your standing at the future judgment will be determined by what you do with the words of Jesus (Matt. 7:24–27).

Only the words of Jesus take the repentant sinner down the narrow way that leads to life. The importance of his words has never expired. They were relevant then and are relevant now. Every day we must ask, "What will I do with the words of Jesus?" We're building our lives on something, and Jesus' words are the only solid foundation for sinners.

PARABLES AND EARS TO HEAR

Not all of Jesus' teachings were easily understood, and this was by design. He didn't mind employing figures and images for things he said, and this kind of language required reflection and insight.

According to Mark 4, Jesus would tell parables to crowds (Mark 4:1–2). A parable was an extended analogy, chiefly about the kingdom of God. He said, "With what can we compare the kingdom of God, or what parable shall we use for it?" (4:30). He would teach about the kingdom with language about a sower and different kinds of soil, a mustard seed and a large tree, dough and leaven, a field with a hidden treasure, a net full of good and bad fish, and other images too.

Jesus' parables were not like sermon illustrations. A preacher intends a sermon illustration to make points clearer. The parables in the Gospels obscure instead of clarifying the nature of the kingdom. Jesus said, "This is why I speak to them in parables, because seeing they do not see, and hearing they do not hear, nor do they understand" (Matt. 13:13), and then he quoted from Isaiah, who indicted a group of people for being spiritually dull and imperceptive (13:14–15; Isa. 6:9–10).

If people understood Jesus' parables, their understanding revealed spiritual insight instead of a hard heart. If people listened to Jesus' parables but didn't grasp the meaning, this lack of insight confirmed their dullness. By teaching in parables, Jesus' words revealed who was "in" and who was still "out."

Jesus told his disciples, "To you has been given the secret of the kingdom of God, but for those outside everything is in parables" (Mark 4:11). Being "outside" was a spiritual condition. The opposite—being "inside"—meant learning and growing in understanding about the kingdom Jesus was proclaiming. When Jesus said, "He who has ears to hear, let him hear" (4:9), he was emphasizing spiritual discernment.

More than physical hearing was necessary. People needed to spiritually perceive what Jesus was teaching. Kingdom truths were discernible to kingdom people, and kingdom people were those who were trusting Jesus and seeking understanding.

SIGNS AND WONDERS

As Jesus traveled to teach, he also performed signs and wonders. Unlike the plagues in the book of Exodus, Jesus' works brought restoration and life. He was a greater Moses leading a new and greater exodus. Jesus' miracles were so vast in scope that the disciple John said they couldn't all be written down (John 20:30–31; 21:25). Readers of the Gospels, then, will only find a small selection of the larger number of wonders that Jesus did during his earthly ministry.

We can divide Jesus' miracles into four categories. Looking at these categories as a whole, we can conclude that nothing lies outside Jesus' authority. He speaks the words of God because he is God, and he subdues what he confronts.

First, Jesus performed *nature miracles*. These include the wonders of Jesus calming the storm on the Sea of Galilee (Mark 4:35–41), feeding thousands with some fish and loaves (6:30–44), and walking on water (6:45–52). In nature miracles, Jesus is exercising dominion over some feature of the physical world.

Second, Jesus performed *exorcisms*. In Mark's Gospel, an exorcism is the first miracle of the book. Jesus' ministry is set in the context of spiritual warfare, and his dominion over principalities and powers is key to his supremacy as the Son of God. He delivered a possessed man in a synagogue (Mark 1:21–28), in Gentile territory (5:1–20), and at the bottom of a mountain (9:14–29). Many exorcisms were not narrated. We read summary statements like Mark 1:39: "And he went throughout all Galilee, preaching in their synagogues and casting out demons."

Third, Jesus performed *physical healings*. When Jesus encountered the sick and the diseased, they left healed and whole. He restored a leper (Mark 1:40–45), the lame (2:1–12), the deaf (7:31–37), and the blind (8:22–26). He healed a man with a withered hand (3:1–6) and a woman who couldn't stop bleeding (5:25–34). People would bring their sick ones to him, and he healed various diseases (1:32–34). No illness proved irreversible. These physical healings confirmed the arrival of God's redeeming work, promised in Isaiah 35: "Then the eyes of the blind shall be opened, and the ears of the deaf unstopped; then shall the lame man leap like a deer, and the tongue of the mute sing for joy" (Isa. 35:5–6).

Fourth, Jesus performed *resurrections*. These resurrections were not like his own resurrection, for he defeated death and was never to die again. When Jesus raised someone from the dead during his earthly ministry, the restoration was to *mortal* life. He raised a young girl (Matt. 9:23–26), a young boy (Luke 7:11–17), and his friend Lazarus from the dead (John 11:38–44). Other unnarrated resurrections may have been part of his earthly ministry as well.

The miracles of Jesus prompted questions about his identity. When he calmed the storm on the sea, the disciples asked, "Who then is this, that even the wind and the sea obey him?" (Mark 4:41). Broaden that question to the other miracles as well. Who then is this, that demons flee and bread multiplies and water becomes wine? Who then is this, that the blind see and the deaf hear and the dead live?

CLAIMS ABOUT HIMSELF

The four Gospels want you to ask about Jesus' identity when you read their accounts and then to believe the answers they give you along the way. Jesus is the Son of David and the Son of Abraham (Matt. 1:1). He is the Christ (Mark 8:29). He is the Son of God (Mark 15:39).

In addition to reporting their own claims about Jesus' identity, the Gospel writers include Jesus' claims about himself. He called himself the Son of Man (Mark 8:31; 9:31; 10:33; 13:26;

14:62). Doing some miracles on the Sabbath, he demonstrated that he was Lord of the Sabbath (2:28). And he made a series of "I am" statements as well.

John's Gospel records seven "I am" statements. Jesus claimed to be the bread of life (John 6:35), the light of the world (8:12), the door of the sheep (10:7), the good shepherd (10:14), the resurrection and the life (11:25), the way, and the truth, and the life (14:6), and the true vine (15:1).

When we look at Jesus' claims, his teachings, and his miracles, truly we are dealing with someone different from and greater than the leaders in the Old Testament. Here is someone speaking with divine authority that isn't derived from God. Here is someone speaking as God. He is the Word made flesh (John 1:1–14). Here is someone who can overcome the effects of sin and the curse upon the world.

The Son of God is God with us, full of power and mercy. He is wiser than Solomon, more glorious than the temple, and greater than the greatest prophet who ever lived. His signs and wonders reveal his glory and confirm his identity. He is the curse-reversing, death-subduing, demon-expelling Christ, the deliverer whom God promised in Genesis 3:15. And in order to accomplish victory over sin and blessing for the nations of the world, he would lay down his life.

LIGHT OF THE SON

In Mark 8, 9, and 10, Jesus taught that the Son of Man would suffer, die, and rise. Amid these teachings was a revelatory event that took place on a mountain and to only a few disciples. In Mark 9:2–13, Jesus was transfigured.

The transfiguration is reported in the Gospels of Matthew, Mark, and Luke. The scene is a revelation of Jesus' glory. Jesus went on a mountain with Peter, James, and John. "And he was transfigured before them, and his clothes became radiant, intensely white, as no one on earth could bleach them" (Mark 9:2–3). The shining was not reflecting *off* Jesus; it was emitting *from* Jesus.

Making the scene even more remarkable, both Moses and Elijah appeared on the mountain and spoke with Jesus (Mark 9:4). A cloud overshadowed them, and a voice called out, "This is my beloved Son; listen to him" (9:7). The Father's words were reminiscent of what he said at the Son's baptism (1:11). These words on the mountain, like the words at the river, were about the Son's identity.

The Old Testament has stories of Moses and Elijah encountering the glory of God on a mountain (Exod. 34:1–9; 1 Kgs. 19:9–18). And here the men are in Mark 9:2–13, speaking with Jesus on a mountain as his glory shines. According to Luke 9:31, they spoke with Jesus about his coming departure (or "exodus"), which would take place in Jerusalem.

The scene ended as suddenly as it had begun (Mark 9:8). The three disciples were left with Jesus, who no longer shone with radiant light. Jesus instructed them not to tell anyone about this until he had risen from the dead (9:9). For the time being, Jesus' sights were on Jerusalem. He had a mission to fulfill, suffering to endure, sins to bear, and death to defeat.

UNDERSTANDING JESUS

- Jesus preached the kingdom of heaven because he inaugurated the long-awaited rule of the Son of David.
- Jesus chose twelve disciples because he was forming a new Israel in the promised land.
- Teaching was a crucial part of Jesus' ministry, but he spoke many things in parables because understanding the nature of the kingdom ultimately required spiritual discernment.
- The miracles of Jesus were kingdom signs that confirmed the truthfulness of his message and the heavenly origin of his authority.

SUGGESTED READING

- Isaiah 35
- Daniel 2:25–45
- Matthew 5–7
- Mark 4:1–33

4

THE PASSION OF THE CHRIST

The four Gospels do not report all the same teachings or all the same miracles, but they all guide their readers toward the week of Jesus' suffering and death. Though Jesus had a multi-year public ministry, the Gospels are not proportionately divided along those years. A substantial portion of the Gospels is devoted to Passion Week, the time from Palm Sunday to Easter Sunday.

When you look at the amount of material in Matthew 21–28, Mark 11–16, Luke 19–24, and John 12–21, you get the sense that these Gospel writers are presenting the final week of Jesus' ministry as the culmination of everything he had previously taught and done because these chapters are at the end of their books.

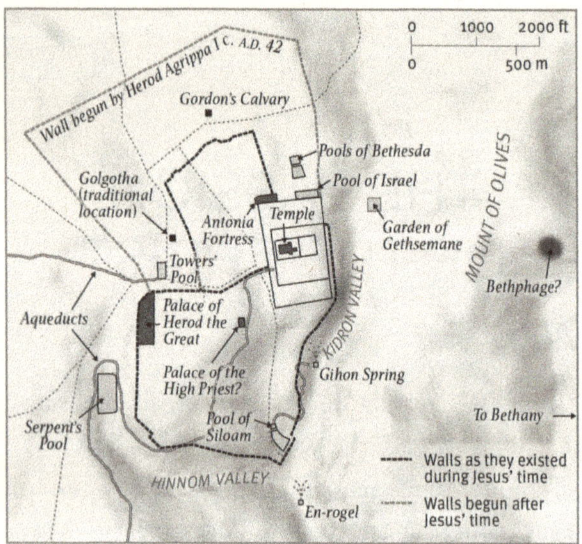

SUNDAY

Though not traveling in a straight line, Jesus "set his face to go to Jerusalem" (Luke 9:51). The timing coincided with the impending Jewish Passover festival, so many pilgrims would be traveling to the city. But on the first day of the week, Jesus' arrival in the city was marked by some significant facts.

Jesus sent two disciples to retrieve a donkey so that he could ride it into Jerusalem. They brought the animal to Jesus, put their cloaks on it, and spread other cloaks on the road, while some people spread branches they had cut from fields (Mark 11:7–8). The whole scene demonstrated acclaim to Jesus, gestures fitting someone of royalty.

And royalty was the key. As Jesus rode on the donkey, those surrounding him were shouting, "Hosanna! Blessed is he who comes in the name of the Lord! Blessed is the coming kingdom of our father David! Hosanna in the highest!" (Mark 11:9–10). The word "Hosanna" means "Save now." The pilgrims' words proclaimed their belief that Jesus was the Son of David who was coming to Jerusalem with salvation in his wake.

The Old Testament is echoed in the scene. According to Zechariah 9, the prophet addressed Jerusalem and said, "Rejoice greatly, O daughter of Zion! Shout aloud, O daughter of Jerusalem! Behold, your king is coming to you; righteous and having salvation is he, humble and mounted on a donkey, on a colt, the foal of a donkey" (Zech. 9:9). In Mark 11, Jerusalem's king was riding to Zion—Jerusalem—on a donkey.

Arriving in the city, Jesus went into the temple and looked around at everything (Mark 11:11). Luke's Gospel tells us that he wept over the city (Luke 19:41). Jesus said, "Would that you, even you, had known on this day the things that make for peace! But now they are hidden from your eyes" (19:42). The city of Jerusalem would be characterized by their rejection of Jesus. Like a prophet of old, Jesus wept over Zion. Spiritually blind, many would not join the acclaim from the crowds that cried out for salvation.

Jesus left the city and went to Bethany, the nearby village where he stayed at night during the week leading up to Passover (Mark 11:11).

MONDAY

On the second day of Passion Week, Jesus journeyed that morning from Bethany to Jerusalem (Matt. 21:17–18; Mark 11:12). He saw a fig tree that didn't have figs and said to it, "May no one ever eat fruit from you again" (Mark 11:14). This pronouncement may seem surprising, even random, but for readers of the Old Testament, a fig tree is associated with *Israel* (Jer. 8:13; 24:1–10; Hos. 9:10).

The fig tree in Mark 11 had no fruit, and Israel did not bear the desirable spiritual fruit. Jesus' action against the fig tree foreshadowed judgment. It suggested divine displeasure toward the fruitless nation. The connection between the fig tree and the rebellious nation is confirmed by what happened after Jesus cursed the tree. He came to Jerusalem and went into the temple.

Entering the temple, Jesus began driving out the buyers and sellers and moneychangers, turning over the tables and seats (Mark 11:15). He rebuked them with words from Isaiah and Jeremiah: "Is it not written, 'My house shall be called a house of prayer for all the nations'? But you have made it a den of robbers" (11:17). In Isaiah 56:7, God's house is called a house of prayer for all people. In Jeremiah 7:11, the prophet indicts his contemporaries for treating the temple like a haven for robbers.

The Son of God in the Jerusalem temple speaks like a fiery prophet, bringing indictments against a wayward people who are heading for judgment. His action of "cleansing the temple" was an acted parable that those with spiritual sight would rightly apply to the spiritual situation of the city. The religious leaders, to some degree, sensed his authority and rebuke. They were seeking a way to destroy him (Mark 11:18).

Jesus' prophetic and parabolic rebuke was followed by acts of healing. The blind and the lame came to him in the temple, and he healed them (Matt. 21:14). These wonderful things didn't soothe the religious leaders; the opposite took place. They were indignant at Jesus' deeds and at the cries of children in the temple: "Hosanna to the Son of David" (21:15).

After these momentous events in the temple, Jesus left the city and returned to Bethany for the night (Mark 11:19).

TUESDAY

On the third day of Passion Week, Jesus returned to the temple, where he had a series of encounters and conversations. In Mark 11–12, these encounters occur in five passages. In each of them, Jesus demonstrated his great wisdom, and he avoided the interrogative traps that certain men with bad motives had set for him.

First, in Mark 11:27 – 12:12, chief priests, scribes, and elders came to Jesus and asked about his authority: "By what authority are you doing these things, or who gave you this authority to do them?" (11:28). Jesus agreed to answer their question if they could tell him whether John the Baptist's baptism practice was from God or from man (11:29–30). They claimed not to know, because they reasoned that answering "from God" would imply that John's message was right, and answering "from man" would put them at odds with the people who held John to be a prophet (11:32–33).

Second, in Mark 12:13–17, some Pharisees and Herodians came "to trap" Jesus in his talk (12:13). The Pharisees were anti-Rome and the Herodians were pro-Rome, so their question to him was carefully crafted: "Is it lawful to pay taxes to Caesar, or not? Should we pay them, or should we not?" (12:14). Jesus' answer was wise and concise: "Render to Caesar the things that are Caesar's, and to God the things that are God's" (12:17). His statement recognized how coins for taxes—which had Caesar's image on them—could rightly be paid to the Roman authorities. His answer didn't alienate the Pharisees or the Herodians. He responded to their question in a way that avoided their trap.

Third, in Mark 12:18–27, a group of Sadducees wanted to show why they thought resurrection hope was a ludicrous doctrine to believe. They came to Jesus with a question about a woman who married a man with seven brothers, and after that man died she married the second brother—eventually working her way through all seven after they each died in turn (Mark 12:19–22). The Sadducees said, "In the resurrection, when they rise again, whose wife will she be? For the seven had her as wife" (12:23). Jesus corrected his skeptics. They had assumed that the life to come would mirror this life, and therefore it would have marriage because this life has marriage. Jesus clarified a discontinuity between the present age and the age to come (12:25). The Sadducees also hadn't considered the power of God, which had been at work in the lives of the patriarchs. Keeping his covenant promises, he is God not of the dead but of the *living* (12:27).

Fourth, in Mark 12:28–34, a scribe approached Jesus and asked, "Which commandment is the most important of all?" (Mark 12:28). Jesus answered by citing Deuteronomy 6:4–5: "The most important is, 'Hear, O Israel: The Lord our God, the Lord is one. And you shall love the Lord your God with all your heart and with all your soul and with all your mind and with all your strength'" (Mark 12:29–30). The most important commandment was not a ceremony, it was not an offering, and it was not a dietary detail. The most important commandment was about loving God. "The second," Jesus said, "is this: 'You shall love your neighbor as yourself.' There is no other commandment greater than these" (Mark 12:31, citing Lev. 19:18).

Fifth, in Mark 12:35–37, though others have asked the questions to this point, Jesus now has a question for them. As he taught in the temple, he asked about David's words in Psalm 110, where David claimed, "The Lord said to my Lord, 'Sit at my right hand, until I put your enemies under your feet'" (Mark 12:36, quoting Ps. 110:1). Reflecting on David's words about the Christ in Psalm 110, Jesus said, "David himself calls him Lord. So how is he his son?" (Mark 12:37). No one was able to answer this question (Matt. 22:46). Jesus asked it in order to highlight a tension in the Old Testament. Calling someone "Lord" was a recognition of higher status and importance. If David (in Psalm 110) called the future king

"Lord," how is that future king David's son? A king's descendant was not automatically considered superior. The resolution to this tension is the incarnation. Because Jesus is the eternal Son, he is David's Lord. And because the Son of God took to himself a truly human nature and was born into the house of David, he is David's son.

After the series of controversial questions and encounters, Jesus left the temple with his disciples and went to the Mount of Olives (Mark 13:3). He pronounced a coming judgment on the temple: "Do you see these great buildings? There will not be left here one stone upon another that will not be thrown down" (13:2).

The generation of the disciples would be the generation that witnessed the temple's destruction (Mark 13:30). Jesus' discourse also prophesied events in the far future. Though Jesus would ascend to the Father, he would return, and his Second Coming would bring resurrection and judgment. The Son of Man's return would be unexpected and sudden (Matt. 24:37–44). When the Son of Man returned in glory, the nations would be gathered through resurrection, and everlasting states would be established through the final judgment (25:31–46).

Jesus would have ended this day like the previous ones that week, by returning to Bethany with his disciples. They had heard him teach with wisdom as well as prophesy with authority. Yet his greatest words and his greatest deeds were still to come.

WEDNESDAY

On the fourth day of Passion Week, Judas agreed to betray Jesus. Mark's Gospel sets the context as "two days before the Passover and the Feast of Unleavened Bread" (Mark 14:1). The day, then, was Wednesday. The religious leaders were trying to figure out how they would seize Jesus, but they were wary of the timing and the people's response (14:1–2).

Judas was the solution to their problem. He "went to the chief priests in order to betray him to them. And when they heard it, they were glad and promised to give him money. And he sought an opportunity to betray him" (Mark 14:10–11). There's no indication that the other disciples knew about this interaction.

According to the biblical record, Judas was the initiator. How strange it must have been for the chief priests when one of the twelve disciples arrived on their doorstep. But they were all too glad to receive him with his plan to betray Jesus. In the list of disciples, the Gospel writers refer to him as Judas Iscariot, "who betrayed him" (Matt. 10:4; Mark 3:19). In Mark 14, Judas' plan materializes, and later in that same chapter it comes to fruition (14:43–45).

No doubt greed was involved. We learn from John's Gospel that Judas was a thief, "and having charge of the moneybag he used to help himself to what was put into it" (John 12:6). But Luke's Gospel adds another, more sinister layer to the plot: "Then Satan entered into Judas called Iscariot, who was of the number of the twelve" (Luke 22:3).

Learning about Judas' plot is devastating. Learning that Satan possessed Judas is terrifying.

THURSDAY

On the fifth day of Passion Week, Jesus ate the last supper. An upper room in a person's house was prepared, and Jesus went there with his disciples (Mark 14:12–16). At a typical Passover meal, the host would speak about the elements on the table and recall the ancient exodus when God delivered the Israelites from Egyptian captivity (Exod. 12:24–27). But during this Passover meal, the disciples heard different words. These words had never been spoken at any Passover meal in the history of the feast.

Jesus took the bread, blessed it and broke it, and then he gave it to his disciples, saying, "Take; this is my body" (Mark 14:22). He took the cup, gave thanks, and then gave it to the disciples for them to drink, saying, "This is my blood of the covenant, which is poured out for many" (14:23–24). Jesus' words about the bread and the cup were about his body and blood, soon to be offered upon the cross.

His words about a covenant did not point backward. They pointed forward to what he would fulfill. Jeremiah 31:31–34 promised a "new covenant," and in Luke 22 Jesus called the cup "the new covenant in my blood" (Luke 22:20). He knew what he had come to accomplish. He was leading a new exodus, and the church of Christ would remember their redemption by keeping the ordinance of the Lord's Supper (22:19; 1 Cor. 11:23–26).

When the last supper ended, they sang a hymn and left for the Mount of Olives (Mark 14:26). There Jesus prophesied the scattering of the disciples, quoting Zechariah 13:7: "You will all fall away," he said, "for it is written, 'I will strike the shepherd, and the sheep will be scattered'" (Mark 14:27). The striking of the shepherd was drawing near, and that meant the scattering of the sheep was at hand.

From the Mount of Olives they traveled to Gethsemane. The hour was late, and the disciples were tired. The time may have even passed midnight. As Jesus prayed to the Father, some of his disciples couldn't remain awake (Mark 14:37–41). Jesus was preparing himself through prayer, and the disciples were unprepared for what lay in store.

Jesus was going to drink the cup of wrath, bearing the judgment for our sins. Picture Gethsemane as a place of temptation. In that garden, the new Adam resolved to obey the will of God: "Yet not what I will, but what you will" (Mark 14:36). The garden of Gethsemane would be a place of the Son's faithfulness and perseverance, his trust and resolve.

Suddenly Jesus told his disciples, "Rise, let us be going; see, my betrayer is at hand" (Mark 14:42). Judas arrived, and with him was a crowd with swords and clubs (14:43). The sign of a kiss would identify Jesus. Judas approached Jesus and said, "Rabbi," and kissed him (14:45). The people with Judas seized the Messiah, prompting Peter to draw his sword and strike a nearby man (John 18:10). But no sword would stop what was unfolding. The time for striking the shepherd had come, and that meant it was time for the sheep to scatter.

"And they all left him and fled" (Mark 14:50).

FRIDAY

On the sixth day of Passion Week, in the early hours of Friday morning, the arresting group took Jesus to the home of Annas, the former high priest (Luke 3:2; John 18:12–13). And then they took Jesus to the home of Caiaphas, the current high priest (Luke 22:54). The purpose of these interactions was for inquiry.

Chief priests, elders, and scribes came together for this occasion (Mark 14:53). A lot of conspiracy and communication had already taken place behind the scenes. The religious leaders wanted the Jewish governing body—known as the Sanhedrin—to render a verdict of blasphemy. False witnesses offered testimony, but their testimony did not agree (14:56).

Intermingled in the Gospel accounts of the Jewish inquiry were Peter's denials in the high priest's courtyard. Peter had followed the entourage to the location, yet he remained outside with others beside a fire (Mark 14:54). When asked if he was one of Jesus' disciples, Peter denied it (14:67–68). He made two additional denials (14:70–71), even swearing an oath that he wasn't the one whom others alleged him to be. When the rooster crowed, Peter broke down in tears, for his denials that night fulfilled the earlier prophecy of Jesus (14:30). Peter fled the courtyard (Luke 22:62).

Inside the residence, the high priest demanded to know, "Are you the Christ, the Son of the Blessed?" (Mark 14:61). Jesus' response was strong and clear: "I am, and you will see the Son of Man seated at the right hand of Power, and coming with the clouds of heaven" (14:62). The high priest tore his own garments and declared those words to be "blasphemy" (14:64). The Sanhedrin pronounced that Jesus deserved death (14:64).

These Jewish proceedings arrived at the desired verdict, but the governing body lacked the authority to administer capital punishment. The Jewish leaders needed to convince the Romans that Jesus was a political threat, and then the Romans could put him to death. Thus began the Roman trials.

Jesus appeared before Pilate (Luke 23:1–5), then before Herod Antipas (23:6–12), and before Pilate again (23:13–17). Neither ruler was convinced that Jesus was guilty of anything deserving death (23:14–15). As was Pilate's custom, he prepared to release a prisoner back to the people, and he asked if they wanted this to be Jesus (Mark 15:6–9). But the crowd instead called for the release of Barabbas, a man who actually was guilty of insurrectionist activity and murder (15:7, 11).

Pilate had Jesus flogged and then crucified (Mark 15:15). Jesus was the suffering Davidic king. He was lifted up on the cross, between two insurrectionists (15:27). He died in Barabbas' place, and that fact made a theological point.

Jesus was dying in the place of sinners. People mocked Jesus, saying, "He saved others; he cannot save himself" (Matt. 27:42). Yet through his death he was bringing salvation. By not saving himself, he was saving others. He was the good shepherd laying down his life for his sheep (John 10:14–15).

Jesus drank the cup of wrath. Darkness covered the land in the afternoon, creating an ominous experience for onlookers (Mark 15:33). Though Jesus looked like any other crucified criminal, he didn't sound like one. He was quoting Psalms (Matt. 27:46), praying for God to forgive his enemies (Luke 23:34), and crying out, "It is finished!" (John 19:30). This was not like any other crucifixion the soldiers had ever seen. When Jesus died, the centurion said, "Truly this man was the Son of God!" (Mark 15:39).

In a way not visible to human eyes, the sinless Son of God became sin for us (2 Cor. 5:21). He was the propitiation of divine judgment (Rom. 3:25). God counted to his Son our sin and shame, that through faith in his Son we might be counted righteous and justified. The cross displayed divine love through the satisfaction of divine justice. God showed his love for us in that while we were still sinners, Christ died on the cross in our place (Rom. 5:8).

Jesus died during the time of day when the Passover lambs were being slain. He was the lamb of God, born to die and take away our sin (Matt. 1:21; John 1:29). As Jesus died, the curtain of the temple split from top to bottom (Matt. 27:51). The atoning death of Jesus fulfilled the purpose of the temple and its sacrificial system. The Son of God was the offering to end all offerings. The veil of his flesh had been torn through crucifixion, and a new covenant would reconcile sinners to the Father through the Son (Heb. 10:19–22).

After Jesus' death, a man named Joseph of Arimathea asked Pilate for the body (Mark 15:42–43). Joseph bought a linen shroud, took Jesus' body from the cross, and prepared him for burial (15:46). He laid the body in a family tomb that had been cut out of rock, and he rolled a stone against the entrance (15:46).

Several women who had seen Jesus' death (Luke 23:49) also witnessed the place where Joseph entombed him (23:55). They planned to return when the Sabbath ended.

SATURDAY

On the seventh day of Passion Week, Pilate dispatched a guard to secure the tomb, since some religious leaders remembered a prediction that Jesus would rise from the dead on the third day (Matt. 27:62–64). Pilate's instructions were simple: "Go, make it as secure as you can" (Matt. 27:65). But all the soldiers in the empire, and all the soldiers of every empire that ever existed, could not have stopped what would happen next.

For now, Jesus rested in peace on the Sabbath day. The stone covered the entrance, the soldiers stood guard, and the disciples were nowhere to be found.

UNDERSTANDING JESUS

- Jesus rode a donkey into Jerusalem because he was the promised king of Zechariah 9:9.
- In the days leading up to Passover, Jesus was teaching in the Jerusalem temple and displaying greater wisdom

than the religious leaders who tried to trap him in his words.

- Upon the cross, Jesus was the suffering king who bore the sins of the people and who fulfilled the institution of the temple and its sacrificial system.
- Dying on the sixth day, Jesus rested in the tomb on the seventh day, keeping the Sabbath.

SUGGESTED READING

- Psalm 22
- Isaiah 52:13 – 53:12
- Matthew 24–25
- Mark 14–15

5

THE TOMB AND THE THRONE

Jesus only needed to borrow Joseph's tomb. On the first day of the week, the body behind the stone awoke. Eyes opened, hands reached for linens, and lungs filled with air. Jesus was bodily alive, but this bodily life was now imperishable.

He had risen from the dead, never to die again. He had risen from the dead so that he could reign forever as the embodied Lord of all.

MORNING RUN

The women who had witnessed Jesus' death and burial went to the tomb toward the dawn of the first day of the week (Matt. 28:1). When they arrived, the stone was already rolled back (Mark 16:4), and no Roman guard was present.

An angel appeared to the women, and he shone like lightning, with clothing as white as snow (Matt. 28:3). He told them, "Do not be afraid, for I know that you seek Jesus who was crucified. He is not here, for he has risen, as he said. Come, see the place where he lay" (28:5–6).

The women confirmed the emptiness of the tomb. We know from later resurrection appearances of the Lord to his disciples that the physicality of walls and boundaries could not obstruct his glorified body. The stone was rolled away not to let our Lord out but to let the women in.

Giving the next piece of instruction, the angel said, "Then go quickly and tell his disciples that he has risen from the dead, and behold, he is going before you to Galilee; there you will see him. See, I have told you" (Matt. 28:7). So the women ran. They went with haste—but also with fear and great joy (28:8).

After coming to the disciples, the women shared the good news. But their words were met with disbelief. The story "seemed to them an idle tale" (Luke 24:11). Nevertheless, Peter rose and ran (24:12), and John—who referred to himself as "the other disciple"—went too (John 20:2–4). They peered inside the tomb and saw that the linen cloths were folded and the face cloth had been set in a place by itself (Luke 24:12; John 20:5–7).

But there was no body to be found. Still not fully understanding what had happened, the disciples went back to their homes.

ON THE ROAD TO EMMAUS

On Sunday—the day Jesus rose from the dead—two people were walking home to a village called Emmaus (Luke 24:13). The subject of conversation was what had happened in Jerusalem—Jesus' condemnation, crucifixion, and present whereabouts (24:14, 19–21).

Jesus drew near to them, and they were kept from recognizing him (Luke 24:15–16). He talked with them as they walked. They told him about what some women had testified:

> *They were at the tomb early in the morning, and when they did not find his body, they came back saying that they had even seen a vision*

> *of angels, who said that he was alive. Some of those who were with us went to the tomb and found it just as the women had said, but him they did not see (24:22–24).*

Their new companion said, "O foolish ones, and slow of heart to believe all that the prophets have spoken! Was it not necessary that the Christ should suffer these things and enter into his glory?" (Luke 24:25–26). Jesus' words pressed the point that the Old Testament prophesied the events which these two travelers had discussed. He began to speak with them about the Old Testament, starting with the books of Moses and then turning to the Prophets, explaining how these Scriptures foretold the Christ (24:27).

Approaching their village, the two people invited Jesus—whom they still didn't recognize—to stay with them for the night. He agreed and joined them for dinner as well. At the table, a remarkable event concluded their time together. He "took the bread and blessed and broke it and gave it to them" (Luke 24:30). This series of actions was reminiscent of the last supper (22:19–20).

While the two Emmaus residents were not of the twelve disciples, they had recently been in Jerusalem (Luke 24:13), and they had been at the specific home with those disciples when the women arrived (24:22–24). No doubt these disciples had spoken of recent things Jesus had said and done, especially the last supper where he had talked about his body and blood with the bread and the cup.

The eyes of the Emmaus witnesses had been "kept from recognizing him" (Luke 24:16), but now "their eyes were opened, and they recognized him" (24:31). They were in their home talking and eating at the table with the risen Jesus. Then, as if this revelation wasn't startling enough, "he vanished from their sight" (24:31).

HIS HANDS AND HIS FEET

That same day, the two Emmaus residents rushed back to Jerusalem, found the eleven gathered together, and told them about the breaking of the bread and the vanishing of Jesus (Luke 24:33–35). Suddenly, needing no door and without any warning, the risen Jesus appeared in the room among them and said, "Peace to you!" (24:36).

According to the Gospel records, this resurrection appearance was to the largest group of people so far. Jesus could tell the disciples were troubled, unsure, confused. He said, "See my hands and my feet, that it is I myself. Touch me, and see. For a spirit does not have flesh and bones as you see that I have" (Luke 24:39).

Jesus' encouragement to touch his hands and feet was a confirmation of his genuine physicality. The disciples did not see a disembodied spirit in the room. They were bearing witness to the risen body of the Jesus they had trusted and followed and most recently abandoned.

Not all the disciples were present for Jesus' appearance. Thomas had not been there. When the others told him about their encounter with Jesus, Thomas said, "Unless I see in his hands the mark of the nails, and place my finger into the mark of the nails, and place my hand into his side, I will never believe" (John 20:25).

A week passed. Then, when the disciples were gathered again and Thomas was with them, Jesus appeared and stood among them (John 20:26). No door was used, yet no wall was an obstacle. Jesus' risen body was capable of doing what their mortal and unglorified bodies could not do.

Jesus told Thomas, "Put your finger here, and see my hands; and put out your hand, and place it in my side. Do not disbelieve, but believe" (John 20:27). Thomas' response was confession and worship: "My Lord and my God!" (20:28).

According to the apostle Paul, Jesus appeared to individuals, small groups, and huge groups (1 Cor. 15:5–8). But because such post-resurrection encounters did not continue after Jesus' ascension (with the exception of Paul in Acts 9), nearly everyone who has followed Jesus as a disciple has not encountered him bodily. We believe without first seeing.

Jesus told his disciples, "Have you believed because you have seen me? Blessed are those who have not seen and yet have believed" (John 20:29). That's you and me, if we trust Christ. Disciples of Jesus are those who have believed in him.

Peter wrote to disciples who hadn't encountered the bodily-risen Jesus. He told them, "Though you have not seen him, you love him. Though you do not now see him, you believe in him and rejoice with joy that is inexpressible and filled with glory, obtaining the outcome of your faith, the salvation of your souls" (1 Pet. 1:8–9).

BREAKFAST BY THE SEA

After Jesus' resurrection, he did not remain physically with his disciples every day. Their pre-cross lives involved frequent interaction with Jesus, but their time with Jesus after his resurrection seemed to be less frequent—though probably more meaningful.

On one occasion, the disciples were fishing in the Sea of Galilee, and Jesus again appeared to them. The disciples hadn't caught anything all night. As day was breaking, Jesus stood on the shore (John 21:3–4) and called to them, "Children, do you have any fish?" (21:5). They didn't, and told him so. "Cast the net on the right side of the boat, and you will find some," he said (21:6).

Without realizing it was Jesus speaking to them, they followed his instruction. They then caught such a huge quantity of fish that they were unable to haul in the net. This whole event recalled an earlier miracle (see Luke 5:1–11). Perhaps that memory helped things click into place for Peter, because John yelled, "It is the Lord!" (John 21:7), and then he jumped into the sea to swim ashore.

When the disciples gathered on the land beside the sea, Jesus was cooking breakfast with fire and fish and bread (John 21:9). When the disciples counted the fish in the net, they numbered 153 large fish—a stunning catch that confirmed a miracle on the water (John 21:11). The disciples had caught nothing during the night, but Jesus' instruction led to an overwhelming haul.

"Come and have breakfast," Jesus said, and the disciples knew it was the Lord who was with them (John 21:12). During this meal, he even took bread and gave it to them (21:13), an action recalling the last supper they'd shared together in an upper room (Luke 22:19).

Jesus was passing out bread and cooking fish on the shore of the sea. What was the significance of this breakfast? Earlier in his ministry, he had taught them that they would be leaving their nets to catch people (Mark 1:17). The fish likely symbolized the Gentile world, the nations. The bread would easily recall the Israelites as a people, because the Lord fed them in the Old Testament with manna from heaven as they journeyed from Egypt to Canaan, and Jesus' miracle of multiplying bread led to twelve baskets of bread being gathered (see Exod. 16:35; Mark 6:43, with the twelve baskets reminding us of the twelve tribes of Israel).

Through breakfast on the beach, Jesus was depicting the mission of his followers. They were to take the good news of Christ to Israel and to the nations.

TEACHING THE OLD TESTAMENT

One of the ways Jesus equipped his disciples to spread the truth about him was by teaching them how the Old Testament prepared the way for his person and work. Everything that had happened was part of God's ordained redemptive plan to bring salvation to the nations.

Jesus told the disciples, "These are my words that I spoke to you while I was still with you, that everything written about me in the Law of Moses and the Prophets and the Psalms must be fulfilled" (Luke 24:44). Jesus was encapsulating the Old Testament books by referring to a threefold division.

The Law, the Prophets, and the Psalms were three categories that denoted the whole Old Testament revelation. The term "Psalms" was a shorthand way of referring to Scripture that was neither the Law (the books of Genesis, Exodus, Leviticus, Numbers, and Deuteronomy) nor the Prophets (some written by actual prophets), but now this third section goes by the term Writings. When scholars and historians refer to the Law, Prophets, and Writings, they're referencing the same sections Jesus invoked with his words.

According to Luke 24:44, the Old Testament anticipated Jesus. Things had been "written about me." These Old Testament prophecies, patterns, and types would reach fulfillment because God inspired the Old Testament documents. Jesus said, "Thus it is written, that the Christ should suffer and on the third day rise from the dead, and that repentance for the forgiveness of sins should be proclaimed in his name to all nations, beginning from Jerusalem" (24:46–47).

If we read the Old Testament correctly, we will see that it is full of promises and expectations that Jesus brought to fulfillment. His suffering, death, and resurrection are prophesied and typified in the Law, Prophets, and Writings. The proclamation of forgiveness and the mission to the nations are also rooted in the Old Testament revelation to God's people.

The disciples then—and now—needed to read the Old Testament through new eyes. Luke's Gospel tells us that Jesus "opened their minds to understand the Scriptures" (Luke 24:45). In order to truly behold the glory and message of the Old Testament, we need spiritual sight. And spiritual sight is a miracle. We need our minds to be opened. Then, with spiritual understanding and boldness, we will proclaim and teach the good news from the Scriptures.

THE GREAT COMMISSION

Jesus tasked his disciples—and those who would come after them—to make disciples from the nations. This "great commission" was given in Matthew 28:18–20. And this commission is the primary mission of the church to this very day.

Jesus grounds the commission in his own sovereignty: "All authority in heaven and on earth has been given to me" (Matt. 28:18). Based on the worldwide sphere of his total sovereignty, Jesus then said, "Go therefore and make disciples of all nations, baptizing them in the name of the Father and of the Son and of the Holy Spirit, teaching them to observe all that I have commanded you. And behold, I am with you always, to the end of the age" (28:19–20).

Faithfully proclaiming Jesus involves calling other people to follow him. The public profession of any disciple's faith is the ordinance of baptism, a ritual endowed with significance because of its picture of death and resurrection. Going under the water denotes death to sin, and emerging from the water denotes new life in Christ (Rom. 6:3–4). The practice of baptism displays the truth about our union with Christ.

New disciples don't know everything they should, and even old disciples never fully achieve perfect understanding of all things. So disciples need to be taught. They need to learn what Christ himself taught, and they must be exhorted to obey the commands of Christ (Matt. 28:20).

The great commission is framed by Jesus' proclamation of his sovereignty (Matt. 28:18) and the promise of his presence (28:20). This promise would not be kept by his physical presence with them. He would soon ascend.

THE ASCENSION

Jesus had spoken to his disciples about his departure, even if they did not fully understand what he meant at the time. His departure would not be an abandonment, however. He would be with them, by the power and presence of the Holy Spirit. He said, "I tell you the truth: it is to your advantage that I go away, for if I do not go away, the Helper will not come to you. But if I go, I will send him to you" (John 16:7).

This Helper is the Holy Spirit. The disciples would have the presence of Christ with them through the Spirit of Christ abiding in them. The Spirit would equip and enable, teach and remind, encourage and guide. Jesus told the disciples, "But when the Helper comes, whom I will send to you from the Father, the Spirit of truth, who proceeds from the Father, he will bear witness about me" (John 15:26).

The physical departure of Jesus is known as his ascension, and the outcome of the ascension is his heavenly reign. The letter of Hebrews refers to his reign in its opening verses. Speaking about Jesus, the author says he "sat down at the right hand of the Majesty on high" (Heb. 1:3). He has been exalted over all things, given the name that is above every name (Phil. 2:9). Seated at the right hand of God, the risen and ascended Christ reigns over all things (Col. 3:1; 1 Cor. 15:25).

Because the New Testament letters teach the heavenly reign of the embodied Son of God, we are able to infer the ascension. But there are two places where the biblical authors narrate this event: in Luke 24:50–51 and Acts 1:9–11.

Both the Gospel of Luke and the book of Acts are volumes written by Luke, and the ascension forms a hinge point in the volumes. Luke's Gospel ends with it, and Acts opens with it.

Jesus lifted his hands and blessed his disciples as he ascended to heaven (Luke 24:50–51). This blessing with upraised hands demonstrated his priestly status. As he ascended, a cloud took him from their sight (Acts 1:9). This narration recalled Daniel 7:13–14, where the Son of Man went with the clouds to the Ancient of Days, a scene of ascent and glory and reign (see Mark 14:62).

If you're like many Bible readers, perhaps you've overlooked the importance of Christ's ascension in the noble effort of giving due attention to events like Jesus' death and resurrection. This neglect, though, is unfortunate. As we rejoice in what Christ has accomplished through his death and resurrection, we should focus as well upon the ascension as the capstone of his earthly victory. The Lord rises from the dead and rises also to heaven. Christ ascends to reign.

The ascension of Jesus is the fulfillment of words David wrote in Psalm 110:1, where God says to the Messiah, "Sit at my right hand, until I make your enemies your footstool." Risen from the dead in glory, the Son of David ascended in glory.

Someone may ask you, "Where is Jesus now?" The answer, in one sense, is that he is present with us by the Holy Spirit. Also true, however, is that the Son of God is seated in heaven, and this position confirms the certainty of his rule and the supremacy of his power.

The Nicene Creed contains the confession that Jesus "ascended into heaven and is seated at the right hand of the Father."

UNDERSTANDING JESUS

- Jesus' risen body was imperishable and immortal, the firstfruits of the resurrection of the dead.
- Though the disciples did not initially understand that Jesus had been raised bodily from the dead, his appearances and instruction to them confirmed the physical nature of his body.

- The disciples learned from Jesus how the Old Testament patterned and prophesied his person and work.
- The ascension of Jesus confirmed the victory of the cross and the empty tomb, for the risen Christ now reigns in heaven with all authority and with the Name that is above every name.

SUGGESTED READING

- Psalm 110
- Daniel 7:13–14
- Hebrews 1:1–4
- Revelation 5

6

THIRTY YEARS OF HOLY ACTS

You and I live in the period after Christ's ascension. The gospel advances under his reign, and he will build his church according to his sovereign authority and wisdom. Many centuries have passed since his heavenly ascension, and there's much to learn about the witness and faithfulness of Christians throughout the ages. But an entire book of the Bible is dedicated to major events in the first-century church as disciples multiplied and the gospel spread.

In the order of New Testament books, the four Gospels are followed by the book of Acts, which narrates selected events in the life of the early church. The years covered in Acts are from the AD 30s to the 60s, so the book spans approximately thirty years. The account of these three decades is not just what early Christians said and did. The book is about what the risen Christ was doing through his early followers. The outpoured Spirit empowered the disciples for witness and for endurance. They faced accusations and persecutions. They traveled and preached. They faced mobs and authorities. They stood before Jewish leaders and Gentile governors.

The book of Acts is Luke's account of how the ascended Jesus built and sustained the early church by the power of the Spirit.

FROM JERUSALEM TO ROME

Before Jesus ascended, he promised his disciples that they would be witnesses near and far, and this promise was a prophecy: "But you will receive power when the Holy Spirit has come upon you, and you will be my witnesses in Jerusalem and in all Judea and Samaria, and to the end of the earth" (Acts 1:8).

The author of Acts is interested in tracking the fulfillment of Acts 1:8. The narrative starts in Jerusalem, moves broader to parts of Judea and Samaria, and ends with Paul in Rome. "To the end of the earth" is represented by the heart of the Roman Empire. The words of Acts 1:8, then, foreshadow the progress of the whole book.

Learning that they would be witnesses for the risen Jesus, the disciples also heard about how they would be empowered for this task. The Holy Spirit would be upon them with power. We should recall the words of John the Baptist, who prophesied that the one coming after him would baptize with the Holy Spirit. Though John had spoken those words a few years earlier, the fulfillment of the promise was near. Jesus said they would "be baptized with the Holy Spirit not many days from now" (Acts 1:5).

In the meantime, the disciples were to remain in Jerusalem, so they returned to that city after Christ's ascension. Since Judas had defected, the disciples cast lots to discern who should be formally added to their small band in order to restore the number twelve. The lot fell on Matthias, and he was then counted among the other eleven apostles (Acts 1:26).

According to the criteria they applied, the candidate for apostleship needed to have been a follower of Christ for a long time, he needed to have been a witness to the risen Jesus, and he needed to be appointed by the Lord. The account in Acts 1:21–26 indicates that Matthias met these criteria. Matthias had been with the disciples since the beginning of Jesus' public ministry, and he had been present when Jesus ascended. The Lord appointed Matthias through the casting of the lot.

Once again a group of twelve, the apostles waited in Jerusalem for the promised Spirit.

A MIGHTY RUSHING WIND

Fifty days after Passover was the day of Pentecost, and on this day the Spirit came. While the disciples were together in one room, they heard a "sound like a mighty rushing wind, and it filled the entire house where they were sitting" (Acts 2:2). The experience was both audible and visual: "And divided tongues as of fire appeared to them and rested on each one of them. And they were all filled with the Holy Spirit and began to speak in other tongues as the Spirit gave them utterance" (2:3–4).

The scene recalled Mount Sinai in Exodus 19, where God's presence descended with power and fire. And the scene recalled the tower of Babel in Genesis 11, where God confused the people's speech and dispersed them. When Luke reports that the Spirit enabled people to speak in "other tongues," we read that people were hearing others in their own native language (Acts 2:6–12). The outpouring of the Spirit in Jerusalem was signaling the reversal of Babel.

Even though the Spirit came upon the disciples in the place they had gathered, the Spirit's work didn't remain there. A glorious outbreak of testimony was happening in Jerusalem, and people from all over the place were together and speaking in the power of the Spirit (Acts 2:9–11). Such a momentous event required public explanation. Peter rose to the occasion. He was different from the man of three denials in the Gospels. Though still Peter, he had been affirmed and commissioned by the risen Christ (see John 21:15–19). The Spirit empowered his presence and filled him with boldness.

Lifting his voice, Peter proclaimed what God had done through this outpouring of the Holy Spirit. "But this is what was uttered through the prophet Joel," he said (Acts 2:16). In Joel 2:28–32, the prophet spoke of a coming day when God would pour out the Spirit "on all flesh" (Joel 2:28). Men and women, young and old, would be filled with the Spirit of God. And according to Peter, the day of Pentecost in Acts 2 was the fulfillment of these ancient words.

Especially important in the passage from Joel which Peter quoted was the promise of salvation: "And it shall come to pass that everyone who calls upon the name of the Lord shall be saved" (Acts 2:21, citing Joel 2:32). The need of the hour was for people to trust Christ as Savior and Lord. Peter proclaimed that Jesus died and rose according to the foreordained plan of God (Acts 2:22–24). Though people in Jerusalem had demanded Jesus' crucifixion, the resurrection and ascension of Christ confirmed his victory and vindication.

Some of the listeners asked the right question: "Brothers, what shall we do?" (Acts 2:37). The proper response to the good news of Christ was to repent and be baptized (2:38). So people responded with repentance and baptism (2:41). The day of Pentecost was a day of salvation. The miraculous experiences of the outpoured Spirit and foreign tongues were signs of the veracity of the gospel message and the kingdom of Christ.

BOLDNESS AND TROUBLE

Signs and wonders characterized not only the earthly ministry of Christ; they continued in the ministry of the apostles (Acts 2:43). In Acts 3:1–10, Peter healed a lame man at a temple gate, and this miracle sparked a series of events. First, Peter gave a speech that indicted people in Jerusalem for killing Jesus, but he also proclaimed the resurrection of Jesus (3:11–16). He called the listeners to repentance (3:19).

Second, while many did believe, some religious leaders intervened, and Peter and

John were arrested (Acts 4:1–4). A hearing was scheduled for the following day. The leaders demanded to know by what name or authority the apostles had acted (4:7). Empowered by the Holy Spirit, Peter proclaimed that Jesus was the rejected stone which was now the cornerstone, and he said that Jesus' name is the name for salvation (4:8–12).

The Jewish leaders warned Peter and John not to speak in the name of Jesus anymore and then released them (Acts 4:18–21). But Peter and John refused to stay silent. The parallel experiences of boldness and opposition pervade many of the Acts narratives. Before Jesus' resurrection, Peter was timid (see Luke 22:54–62); now Peter was bold. In Acts he is willing to defy the authorities and face arrest for his preaching.

The healing of the lame man was obvious, so the religious leaders could not deny the miracle (Acts 4:16). But they wanted to suppress the spread of Jesus' name. The establishment had recently crucified the man, yet the followers of Jesus now seemed bolder than ever. In fact, the apostles prayed for courage: "And now, Lord, look upon their threats and grant to your servants to continue to speak your word with all boldness, while you stretch out your hand to heal, and signs and wonders are performed through the name of your holy servant Jesus" (4:29–30).

Wonders continued. As in the days of Jesus' earthly ministry, when the Gospel writers gave brief summary statements of widespread healings, Luke tells us in Acts 5:12: "Now many signs and wonders were regularly done among the people by the hands of the apostles." People were trusting Christ, and the church grew.

The miracles confirmed the authority of the apostles, and these miracles were reminiscent of what Jesus himself performed in the Gospel accounts (Acts 5:14–16). The miracles included exorcisms, for the ministry of the apostles was pushing back the darkness with the light of Jesus' name (5:16; see also 8:6–7).

Spiritual boldness brought social and religious trouble. In light of the preaching and healing done by the apostles, the religious leaders arrested them again and put them in prison (Acts 5:17–18). An angel of the Lord delivered them from prison and told them to keep preaching the words of life (5:19–20).

The boldness of the apostles in the book of Acts has been an inspiration through the centuries of the church, because the spread of the gospel inevitably meets opposition and persecution. Yet the words of the apostles bring clarity to the priority we should have when mobs or authorities forbid the preaching of Christ: "We must obey God rather than men" (Acts 5:29).

That conviction remains relevant today because our modern world resists the authority of Christ. This resistance can manifest as revilement against believers. Have you faced mockery from friends or family members because of your beliefs? Have you endured threats or even violence for the sake of the gospel? Have you been on the receiving end of conniving plans by which others seek your demise because of your courage to stand for what is true?

The importance of the gospel is worthy of boldness from its confessors.

THE STONING OF STEPHEN

The escalation of persecution led to martyrdom in Acts 6–8. A man named Stephen was performing miracles and speaking with wisdom (Acts 6:8–10), but some people believed he committed blasphemy (6:11). They stirred up a mob that included elders and scribes, and false witnesses spoke against Stephen (6:12–14).

When the time came for Stephen to address the charges, he gave a lengthy speech that overviewed Israel's history. He spoke of the patriarchs and divine promises (Acts 7:1–16). He reviewed the life of Moses and the exodus of the Israelites (7:17–36). He also emphasized the obstinance and disobedience of that wilderness generation (7:37–43).

The hardheartedness of those ancient stiff-necked people echoed in the hardheartedness of Stephen's accusers. He told them,

> *You stiff-necked people, uncircumcised in heart and ears, you always resist the Holy Spirit. As your fathers did, so do you. Which of the prophets did your fathers not persecute? And they killed those who announced beforehand the coming of the Righteous One, whom you have now betrayed and murdered, you who received the law as delivered by angels and did not keep it (Acts 7:51–53).*

Stephen accused his accusers. He labeled them guilty of resisting the Spirit, persecuting those whom God raised up, and murdering the Messiah. They were insolent lawbreakers. Ultimately their problem was spiritual: they were "uncircumcised in heart and ears." They would not have conceived of themselves as unbelievers and rebels, yet their actions confirmed this very identity.

The mob raged against Stephen (Acts 7:54). In opposing Stephen, they were opposing Christ. As the seed of the serpent, they persecuted the seed of the woman. They took Stephen outside the city and stoned him (7:58). As he was dying, Stephen said, "Lord Jesus, receive my spirit" (7:59), and, "Lord, do not hold this sin against them" (7:60). These dying words of Stephen remind us of the dying words of Jesus. On the cross, Jesus had said, "Father, into your hands I commit my spirit" (Luke 23:46), as well as, "Father, forgive them, for they know not what they do" (23:34). Stephen died with the words of Christ on his lips.

The martyrdom of Stephen was the catalyst for a persecution against the church that resulted in the scattering of disciples throughout the regions of Judea and Samaria (Acts 8:1), and this scattering enabled greater obedience to the Great Commission (Matt. 28:19–20; Acts 1:8).

Stephen's death prompted some devout men to bury his body and lament his murder (Acts 8:2). But not everyone mourned Stephen's death. A man named Saul approved of his execution (8:1). Saul was a fierce persecutor of the church, and he made every effort to suppress the Christian movement. He traveled house to house, targeting not only Christian families living there but also churches meeting there (8:3). He wanted Christian men and women in prison, and hopefully the outcome would be the decline and extinguishment of these Jesus followers.

On one occasion, Saul went to the high priest asking for official letters to Jewish synagogues at Damascus. He intended to arrest any Christians he found and then return with them to Jerusalem (Acts 9:1–2). But the Saul who arrived in Damascus would be a different Saul than the one who started down that road.

ON THE ROAD TO DAMASCUS

Acts 9 is a pivotal point in the book because it tells the story of Saul's conversion. While traveling to Damascus to apprehend Christians, suddenly a blinding light shone around him (Acts 9:3). He heard a voice say, "Saul, Saul, why are you persecuting me?" (9:4). This was the voice of the risen Messiah: "I am Jesus, whom you are persecuting" (9:5).

With that revelation, Saul's life turned upside down. He had been an Israelite, of Benjamin's tribe in particular (Phil. 3:5). He had been a devoted Hebrew, a zealous Pharisee, an avid keeper of the law (3:5–6). And in his misguided zeal, he had opposed the church of Jesus because he believed that Jesus was a fraud, a disqualified Messiah.

Saul the persecutor would be known as Paul the apostle (Acts 13:9; 1 Cor. 15:8–9). Though Saul was his Jewish name, Paul was likely a Roman name he possessed from birth, since he was a Roman citizen (Acts 22:25). His name Paul would be especially useful as he ministered to the Gentiles. The Lord chose Saul to be an instrument for the spread of the gospel, to take Christ's name before "Gentiles and kings and the children of Israel" (9:15).

In a later reflection on his conversion, Paul wrote that "formerly I was a blasphemer, persecutor, and insolent opponent. But I received mercy because I had acted ignorantly in unbelief, and the grace of our Lord overflowed for me with the faith and love that are in Christ Jesus" (1 Tim. 1:13–14). As Paul describes his life before Christ, he did not evaluate it positively. He had lived with a diehard commitment against the people of Jesus, and he learned that Jesus took persecution personally (Acts 9:1–4).

From his conversion in Acts 9, Paul became zealous for the gospel to such a degree that he was prepared to endure persecution, prison, and death. As he journeyed and preached, Jews and Gentiles came to know Christ. He didn't limit his travels to the land of Israel. He conducted missionary journeys that took him many miles and ultimately led him to Rome itself.

After Acts 9, the remainder of the book is mainly about the apostle Paul's ministry. Luke's selective account of Paul's missionary journeys is appropriate because of how great a role Paul played in the spread of the gospel to his first-century generation of Jews and Gentiles.

MISSIONARY JOURNEYS

Paul's travels in Acts can be grouped into three missionary journeys, because on three occasions he launched ventures from a city called Syrian Antioch.

The first missionary journey begins in Acts 13:1–3 and ends in 14:24–28. The second missionary journey begins in 15:36 and ends in 18:22. The third missionary journey begins in 18:23 and ends in 21:17. This third journey doesn't end with Paul returning to Syrian Antioch; it ends when the authorities arrested Paul while he was in Jerusalem (21:30–33).

These three journeys took place from approximately AD 46 to 57. Throughout the many miles Paul traveled, he ministered with coworkers, planted churches, encouraged existing churches, and endured persecution. When you read through Acts 13 to 21 (during which his missionary journeys unfold), you'll notice that his travels are outside the promised land as he takes the gospel into Asia and Europe.

A key feature in the record of Paul's journeys—and also a key feature earlier in Acts—is speeches. Paul's speeches address the spiritual needs of his listeners as he explains the message of Christ crucified and risen. Whether addressing a Jewish mob or Gentile pagans, whether speaking to authorities or to regular citizens of a region, Paul knew how to magnify Christ in the given situation. It was not unusual for Paul to be in a synagogue on the Sabbath day, proclaiming that Jesus is the Christ and explaining from the Old Testament how it was so (Acts 17:2).

The ministry of Paul was characterized by miracles as well as teaching, just like the ministry of Peter. According to Acts 19:11–12, "God was doing extraordinary miracles by the hands of Paul, so that even handkerchiefs or aprons that had touched his skin were carried away to the sick, and their diseases left them and the evil spirits came out of them." In Acts 20:7–12, a young man named Eutychus died and was raised from the dead. These wonders confirmed the authority and veracity of Paul's ministry. The living Christ was working through this apostle.

The missionary ventures of Paul were not solo endeavors. When you read the book of Acts alongside the New Testament letters, it is evident that Paul operated with a network of individuals. He coordinated plans, dispatched coworkers, wrote letters to provide instructions, and traveled with others who could support the ministry with their friendship, wisdom, resources, and devotion.

UNDER ARREST

Paul's third missionary journey came to a standstill when the authorities arrested him in Jerusalem (Acts 21:33). His arrest in Jerusalem was a pivotal point in the Acts narratives. In Acts 24, he testified before Governor Felix in Caesarea (Acts 24:1–21). Paul remained in Caesarean custody for two years (24:27).

A man named Festus was the successor to Felix, and Paul appeared before Festus too (Acts 25:1–12). Paul's appeal to Caesar—knowing that this was part of the Lord's plan for him to testify in Rome (23:11)—meant that a journey to Rome began (27:1). The remainder of Acts tells of this trip. It wasn't smooth, as it involved a shipwreck along the way, but eventually he came to Rome (28:16).

The book of Acts doesn't narrate Paul's appearance before the emperor in Rome. It ends with him still under house arrest. He was there two years (Acts 28:30), from approximately AD 60 to 62. He was able to receive visitors (28:23, 30), and he leveraged this time to proclaim Christ with boldness (28:31). Though Paul was bound, the gospel was unbound. Though he was under arrest, the unchained gospel continued to spread to the lost by the power of the living Christ.

UNDERSTANDING JESUS

- Jesus baptized his followers with the Holy Spirit when he poured the Spirit upon them on the day of Pentecost.
- The miracles of the apostles were like the ones Jesus performed during his earthly ministry, and this continuity confirmed the power and work of the ascended Christ through his followers.
- Jesus promised his followers that they would face hardship and persecution, and the narratives in Acts report the fulfillment of his words in the early church.

- Saul the persecutor encountered the risen and exalted Christ, and his conversion led to many years of mission work for the spread of the gospel among the nations.

SUGGESTED READING

- Psalm 106
- Joel 2:28–32
- Galatians 1:11–24
- 1 Timothy 1:12–17

7

LETTERS FOR THE WAY

When you flip through the pages of the New Testament, you'll be going through a lot of mail. The New Testament contains twenty-seven books, and twenty-one of them are letters (or epistles). Not all of the letters are from the same author, but they are all written for specific purposes—some letters to churches and others to individuals.

If we're going to understand the story of the New Testament, we need to consider what information the letters contribute. The following reflections won't give a thorough overview of each letter. But they will offer ways we should think about these letters as a whole.

The letter-writers are building up the readers in the Christian faith. They are directing them in how to understand and keep in step with the good news of the gospel. Though we are not the initial recipients of these epistles, we are the present audience. The unchanging doctrinal truths and applications are relevant for our discipleship.

THE ORDER OF THE LETTERS

Of the twenty-one New Testament letters, thirteen are from the apostle Paul, and these appear in a group right after the book of Acts. The placement of these thirteen letters makes sense, because the book of Acts ends with the apostle Paul. Acts 28, then, is followed by Paul's thirteen letters.

Paul's letters divide into two groups: nine letters to churches and four to individuals. Romans through 2 Thessalonians are letters to churches, and 1 Timothy through Philemon are to individuals. Within these two groups, the order is longest to shortest. Ordering the letters by size means that the letters aren't ordered according to date of composition. In group one, Romans is the longest, and the size decreases through 2 Thessalonians. In group two, 1 Timothy is the longest letter, and the size decreases through Philemon—this last letter being the shortest of all Pauline epistles.

After these thirteen letters of Paul is a series of eight letters that aren't for any one location or any one individual. The letters seem rather general, and are therefore sometimes called the General Epistles. They comprise the writings from Hebrews to Jude. And for the most part they are organized from longest to shortest (an exception being James and 1 Peter, for the former is shorter than the latter).

AUTHORS OF THE LETTERS

In terms of authorship of New Testament letters, we've already considered Paul's name, since the thirteen letters after Acts are from him. He is the former persecutor of the church, the man Saul of Tarsus, the one whom Christ called to be an apostle. He consistently begins his letters by identifying himself as the author.

There is no compelling reason to doubt Paul's authorship of the letters which bear his name. While we should not presume that we have all the letters Paul ever wrote, we do have the thirteen which the Holy Spirit has inspired and preserved for the church of Jesus Christ. The titles of these thirteen letters are based on the recipients, whether written to churches in cities or regions (like Philippi or Galatia) or to individuals (like Titus or Philemon).

At the head of the General Epistles, the letter of Hebrews is technically anonymous, because there is no opening authorship claim. Scholars have sometimes suggested an author such as Paul or Apollos or Luke, and one of those names may be correct, but we cannot be sure.

James is an epistle named not for its recipient but for its author. In the General Epistles, the letters with names (James, Peter, John, Jude) are letters written by those men. Church tradition holds that the letter of James is from Jesus' brother and not one of the twelve disciples. Jesus' brother James became a Christian after Jesus' resurrection.

From Peter we have two letters. This Peter is the same man whom Jesus summoned by the Sea of Galilee. This is the same Peter who followed Jesus, confessed "You are the Christ," and later denied even knowing Jesus. Encountering the risen Jesus, however, changed him. The book of Acts records the post-resurrection boldness of Peter as he proclaimed the Messiah.

The letters of 1, 2, and 3 John were likely written by John the apostle. Though the letters are technically anonymous, the testimony of early church tradition points to John the apostle as their author. When these letters are read together, they are coherent in terms of style and concerns, and they complement John's Gospel as well. Interpreters rest on reliable evidence in affirming the apostle John as the author of these three letters.

The twenty-first letter is from Jude. According to church tradition, this Jude was the brother of Jesus and became a follower of Jesus after the resurrection. The opening of the letter also identifies him as the brother of James, which would be a reference to the James we've mentioned above, who wrote the letter that bears his name. Among Jesus' siblings, both James and Jude wrote letters that ended up in the New Testament.

RECIPIENTS OF THE LETTERS

The letter-writers had believers in mind as the recipients, and some of the writers named these recipients in the opening greetings. In the group of Paul's letters written to churches, he specifies the cities and regions. We find things like "To all those in Rome" (Rom. 1:7), "To the church of God that is in Corinth" (1 Cor. 1:2), "To the churches of Galatia" (Gal. 1:2), and "To all the saints in Christ Jesus who are at Philippi, with the overseers and deacons" (Phil. 1:1).

Paul's letters are traditionally known by the recipients, including his letters to individuals. He wrote, "To Timothy" (1 Tim. 1:2), "To Titus" (Titus 1:4), and "To Philemon our beloved fellow worker and Apphia our sister and Archippus our fellow soldier, and the church in your house" (Phlm. 1–2).

The letter of Hebrews doesn't specify its recipients. Given the content of the letter, the readers are likely believers who have come from a Jewish background and will face the temptation—in the face of suffering—to revert back to Jewish ways and forsake the Lord Jesus.

Like Hebrews, the letter of James is also general. After James identifies himself as the author, he writes "To the twelve tribes in the Dispersion" (Jam. 1:1). The number "twelve" recalls that there were twelve tribes of Israel. James writes the way he does to address the *new* Israel, the scattered people of God. His letter isn't aiming at one city or region.

The recipients of Peter's two letters are not specific (1 Pet. 1:1; 2 Pet. 1:1). In the first letter, he's writing to believers, describing them as "exiles" throughout Asia. In the second, he's writing "To those who have obtained a faith of equal standing with ours by the righteousness of our God and Savior Jesus Christ." Again, general believers are in view.

In addition to lacking a claim of authorship, 1 John doesn't mention recipients either. We may assume a general audience. The same assumption holds true for 2 John, which opens like this: "The elder to the elect lady and her children" (2 John 1). This "lady" is probably a metaphor for the church, and "her children" would be those who belong to the church. No specific church is named in the letter, however. John's third letter is from "The elder to the beloved Gaius" (3 John 1), so a specific person is in view.

Jude begins his letter by identifying himself as the author and then saying, "To those who are called, beloved in God the Father and kept for Jesus Christ" (Jude 1). Even though the content addresses some specific concerns, Jude doesn't name an individual recipient, nor does he mention a particular city or region. The letter of Jude fits within the larger group of General Epistles.

THE COMPOSITION OF THE LETTERS

The twenty-one New Testament letters were written by six different authors—Paul, the author of Hebrews, James, Peter, John, and Jude—in less than fifty years. Letters like Galatians and James are sometimes dated in the late 40s, and letters like 1, 2, and 3 John are sometimes dated in the 90s.

While these twenty-one letters are rightly ascribed to these various authors, readers should keep in mind a customary practice for letter-writing in Paul's day. Writers could use an *amanuensis*—a secretary who did the actual penning of a letter. Paul's authorship wasn't undermined when he communicated his message through someone else who penned the letter. In Romans, the amanuensis discloses himself: "I Tertius, who wrote this letter, greet you in the Lord" (Rom. 16:22). And yet the opening of Romans—"Paul, a servant of Christ Jesus"—identifies Paul as the sender and author. In other words, we shouldn't think of Romans as the letter from Tertius to the church in Rome. It is Paul's letter to the Roman Christians.

When Paul lists a co-sender beside his name in the opening line of a letter, this co-sender may also be involved in its composition. For instance, the opening of 1 Corinthians says, "Paul, called by the will of God to be an apostle of Christ Jesus, and our brother Sosthenes" (1 Cor. 1:1). Sosthenes may have been Paul's amanuensis for the letter we call 1 Corinthians. To the Philippians, Paul began like this: "Paul and Timothy, servants of Christ Jesus" (Phil. 1:1). Timothy's name may be alongside Paul's to suggest that he is involved in both the sending and composition of the letter to Philippi.

Sometimes the ending of Paul's letters will specify his personal handwriting, indicating his involvement in the letter's message and composition. In Galatians 6:11 he says, "See with what large letters I am writing to you with my own hand." And in 2 Thessalonians 3:17, "I, Paul, write this greeting with my own hand. This is the sign of genuineness in every letter of mine; it is the way I write."

Considering Paul's letters alongside the book of Acts, we can make projections as to how their composition related to his missionary journeys. Based on a series of historical and textual factors, the following order seems sound and compelling: he wrote Galatians after his first missionary journey; 1 and 2 Thessalonians during his second missionary journey; 1 and 2 Corinthians and Romans during his third missionary journey; Ephesians, Philippians, Colossians, and Philemon while under house arrest in Rome; and, finally, 1 and 2 Timothy and Titus sometime after the end of Acts.

STANDARD FEATURES IN THE LETTERS

Since letter-writers existed in the ancient world before Paul, scholars have compared the design of the New Testament letters with those outside the New Testament. Several conventional elements in first-century letters are noteworthy.

First, letters opened with the author's name. Modern letter-writing concludes with the writer. Paul, James, Peter, John, and Jude all put their names in the opening words of their letters. Keeping this convention, the authors added language that further identified themselves or that described themselves with a term like "servant" or "apostle."

Second, the recipient(s) followed the name of the writer. If Paul was writing to the church in Rome or in Corinth, or to an individual like Timothy or Philemon, he clarified these recipients near the beginning of the letter.

Third, after the author and the recipients is a greeting. The conventional first-century letter would have a greeting from the gods. The biblical authors took a standard Gentile greeting (which was similar to the word for "grace") and a Jewish greeting (Shalom, or "peace") and combined them. Paul consistently wished *grace and peace* to his readers near the beginning of his letters. He also mentions that this grace and peace is from God the Father and the Lord Jesus. This emphasis is another example of Paul taking a conventional element of a first-century letter and filling it with theological significance.

Fourth, at this point in the layout of ancient letters, some kind of blessing or thanksgiving would appear. Likewise, the biblical authors include a blessing unto the Lord or a reason for thanksgiving to the Lord. Paying attention to what Paul says in a thanksgiving section is important, because certain themes or words in that section may foreshadow what he expounds in the body of the letter.

Fifth, the opening sections of the letter eventually lead to the body—the place where the letter's chief concerns and arguments are found. The body of the letter would be the longest part of the letter, and that fact is certainly true for the biblical authors in their letters. The body could contain one main idea or a series of issues that the author wanted to address.

Sixth, when the writer completes the main argument(s) of the letter, the conclusion is the obvious last conventional element. The biblical authors use the conclusion section to give travel directives, offer greetings to and from certain people, and make practical requests.

When we are aware of the conventional elements of a first-century letter, any elaboration on or deviation from those elements is noteworthy. As previously mentioned, the opening greetings from Paul would often include additional phrases or terms that endowed the opening verses with theological significance and that foreshadowed themes or arguments that he would address in the body of the letter. Sometimes he would bypass a conventional element entirely, such as in his letter to the Galatians, which lacks a thanksgiving. The letters of Hebrews and 1 John lack an opening claim of authorship and an identification of recipients. And 1 John does not have a typical conclusion.

So while the letters of the biblical authors appropriated conventional forms and features that their contemporaries used, interpreters will notice that these letters do not necessarily contain every form and feature mentioned above.

THE THEOLOGY OF THE LETTERS

A letter is only one side of a conversation, and we don't have the other side. There are inferences we must draw as interpreters. This strategy of "mirror reading" is unavoidable, and we must be willing to make plausible suggestions as to the context, circumstances, and purpose(s) of the letter.

The biblical letters are sometimes called "occasional writings" because a specific occasion or situation has prompted the biblical author to write. While some letters are not to a specific person or city, there are still reasons for the letter's composition, and these reasons must be discerned carefully through a study of the letter's content.

All of the New Testament letters exist to help us know God and to follow him faithfully. These letters teach theology. Some of the letters, especially Paul's, are divided in such a way that doctrinal matters are first, followed by sections of practical instruction and application.

The biblical writers teach about such doctrinal topics as the person of Christ, the sovereignty of God, the nature of the church, and the end times. An author may speak about general gospel truths for readers whom he doesn't know well or at all, while other times the author will answer specific questions or concerns that his recipients have raised.

Old Testament passages pervade the New Testament letters. The biblical authors quote and allude to the Old Testament books in order to make arguments and apply their points. The authors are saturated in the Old Testament, and their writings provide examples of interpreting Scripture that we can study and imitate. The authors see Christ in the Old Testament in prophecies and types. They discern moral lessons from characters and events. They explain the fulfillment Christ has brought to earlier promises and covenants. The New Testament authors help us learn to more faithfully read and interpret the Old Testament as Christians.

A major concern among the letter-writers was the presence of false teaching in the midst of the readers. False teaching undermines sound doctrine, obscures the glory of the gospel, and harms people. Paul, in particular, wanted false teaching confronted and stopped. He knew that people posing as sound teachers would seek to mislead others for the sake of monetary gain and power. False teaching was not only dangerous; it was damnable. He told the Galatians, "But even if we or an angel from heaven should preach to you a gospel contrary to the one we preached to you, let him be accursed" (Gal. 1:8).

All of the New Testament letters, to some degree, instructed the recipients in Christian obedience. As the gospel spread and as people planted churches, believers needed guidance on Christian living, on ethical reasoning. The letters addressed all manner of different discipleship topics. Whether their topic was work or marriage or sexuality or money or suffering or speech or prayer or matters of conscience, the biblical authors sought to help their readers turn from sin and walk in wisdom.

INTERPRETATION OF THE LETTERS

We are many years removed from the recipients of the twenty-one New Testament letters. Yet the theology they teach is necessary for our spiritual growth as well. The ethical matters have not expired but are pertinent to our present discipleship. The letters help us read the Old Testament better, and we are more anchored in the truth of the gospel because of them.

Not being the initial readers of these letters, we have the gap of time and customs to bridge. Scholars discuss which matters in the letters may have been contextually relevant back then but don't apply in the same way now. Debates involve separating culturally-specific customs from the principles which would be applicable across generations and cultures.

We want to avoid the error of minimizing the authority of the writers when we compare their work to the four Gospels. Because the apostles write in the authority of Christ Jesus, their letters bear the same authority as the four Gospels. We should not pit Paul against Jesus or Jesus against James or Jude against Peter. The same Holy Spirit who inspired the four Gospels inspired the twenty-one letters, and these letters guide us in wisdom. The letters are the words of Christ to us through his apostles.

The apostles do not mislead us, nor do they contradict one another. We should read the New Testament letters as a harmonious group, knowing that their words may supplement or expand upon what is written elsewhere.

Not all parts of the New Testament letters are easily understood. But as we read and study these ancient pieces of correspondence, we will marvel at the ways the Christ was building and sustaining his church in the first century. We will read warnings we should heed. We will receive imperatives we should follow. And we will learn that the "grace and peace" that begins these letters is far more than a customary greeting.

Grace and peace are what make and shape the Christian life.

UNDERSTANDING JESUS

- The writings of the apostles bear the authority of Christ himself, so we should not read the letters as if they are less authoritative than other biblical books.
- Jesus teaches and edifies his people through the letters which churches and individuals received.
- The gospel of Christ must be proclaimed and defended, lest false teaching obscure the truth of the gospel and confuse the people of God.
- Living in Christ and for Christ will mean bringing the various areas of our lives in subjection to his lordship, and the biblical wisdom of the New Testament letters is aiming at this goal.

SUGGESTED READING

- Jeremiah 29:1–23
- Daniel 4
- Romans 1:1–17
- 2 Peter 3:14–18

8

HOPE FOR ALL THE EARTH

The end of the New Testament story is the end of the whole Bible's story. Revelation has a reputation of difficulty because its primary genre is visionary and apocalyptic, and this kind of writing employs many symbols and images that can be notoriously challenging to interpret.

John's Apocalypse is a book for the imagination because it helps us to picture the horrors of divine judgment, rejoice in the glory of new creation, and feel the urgency to follow Christ instead of the worldly powers of this evil age.

TO SEVEN CHURCHES

The opening chapter of Revelation says that its audience is seven churches in Asia (Rev. 1:4). These churches are specifically addressed in Revelation 2–3, in this order: Ephesus, Smyrna, Pergamum, Thyatira, Sardis, Philadelphia, and Laodicea. These seven cities do not exhaust the application and purpose of the book, because the number "seven" in Scripture often portrays completeness. The seven churches in Asia probably symbolize the churches of Christ everywhere.

John the apostle wrote to these churches sometime during the final decades of the first century. Believers were facing opposition and hostility for their faith, false teachers were causing havoc, and some professing Christians had grown lukewarm with regard to their love for Christ. The first few chapters of Revelation are about a vision of Christ who gives words of warning and encouragement to these churches.

Jesus is the first and the last, the alpha and the omega. As the one who holds the keys of death, his rule and authority should compel the obedience of his disciples and the fear of his enemies. He calls his people to a life of faithfulness, and he promises the crown of life for those who endure (Rev. 2:10–11). Suffering will tempt believers to compromise. The cost of discipleship may cause them to grow weary and lose heart.

The Lord promised his people, "The one who conquers and who keeps my works until the end, to him I will give authority over the nations, and he will rule them with a rod of iron, as when earthen pots are broken in pieces, even as I myself have received authority from my Father" (Rev. 2:26–27). Jesus' promise alludes to Psalm 2:8–9, which spoke of the Messiah's reign over the nations. Revelation 2:26–27 uses the imagery of Psalm 2 to describe the reign of the saints. As the book of Revelation makes clear, the people of Christ will reign *with* Christ.

THE LAMB WHO REIGNS

The hope of future reign for the saints is based on the truth of the present reign of Christ. He is even now both Lord and Christ. He possesses all authority in heaven and on earth. He is seated at the right hand of God in the heavenly places.

Revelation 5 describes the reign of Christ. He is the one worthy to open the scroll in 5:2–5.

One of the heavenly elders said to John, "Weep no more; behold, the Lion of the tribe of Judah, the Root of David, has conquered, so that he can open the scroll and its seven seals" (5:5). John saw this lion of Judah, who was also a Lamb that had been slain (5:6). The visionary language is unmistakably about the triumphant Messiah.

Only the authority of the ascended Christ can strengthen believers who must endure suffering for the name of Christ. They can persevere in their hour of trial because the Son of Man holds the scroll and is worthy of worldwide worship and honor. The way of exaltation is through the cross, and this path of suffering to glory is the one that God's people will walk as well. Through the death of Christ, ransomed people have been made a kingdom and priests, and they shall reign on the earth (Rev. 5:9–10).

The present reign of the slain lamb will motivate believers to hold fast to their confession and to their Lord. They need a vision of this glorious truth to help them combat the lies of the world. The way of the cross leads to resurrection, and resurrection leads to everlasting reign. Evil rises now, but it shall fall before the reigning Christ.

Revelation—in sync with the earlier New Testament books—portrays the reign of Christ as inaugurated. The ministry and victory of Christ was the inauguration of this reign. But we await the consummation of all that it means for Jesus to be both Lord and Christ. So believers live between the advents of Christ, between his first coming and his second, between inauguration and consummation.

And while the lamb reigns, a dragon rages.

A RAGING DRAGON

The people of God face suffering in a fallen world, as well as their own besetting sins and frailties. In addition to these things, the malice of the evil one affects God's image-bearers. Satan has an unabating hatred for the people of God. In Revelation 12, this opposition takes the form of a dragon who opposes Christians.

The dragon is "that ancient serpent, who is called the devil and Satan, the deceiver of the whole world" (Rev. 12:9). These words in the Bible's last book remind us of the Bible's first book. In Genesis 3, the evil serpent came into the garden of Eden with deceptive and manipulative words. And he has been the adversary of God's people ever since the fateful fall of Adam and Eve.

The victory of Jesus on the cross was a defeat of the evil one. In John's Gospel, Jesus spoke of this world's ruler being "cast out" (John 12:31). Through his death Jesus would "destroy the one who has the power of death, that is, the devil" (Heb. 2:14). In Revelation 12, we read about this great dragon or serpent being "thrown down" (12:9). This defeat was not a final defeat, however. The final judgment of Satan was still future.

According to Revelation 12:17, "the dragon became furious with the woman and went off to make war on the rest of her offspring, on those who keep the commandments of God and hold to the testimony of Jesus." The offspring or seed of the woman refers to the church. The fury of the devil is toward believers. Part of what stirs his rage is something he knows: "the devil has come down to you in great wrath, because he knows that his time is short!" (12:12).

The devil is not ignorant of what is in store for him. His rage against the church will not ultimately prevail. He will face judgment from the lamb who was slain but who now reigns as the lion of Judah. Jesus taught, "I will build my church, and the gates of hell shall not prevail against it" (Matt. 16:18). While it is true that we wrestle against "the rulers, against the authorities, against the cosmic powers over this present darkness, against the spiritual forces of evil in the heavenly places" (Eph. 6:12), we do so as a people who will reign with Christ. Our future is victory, but that is not the future of the dragon. And thus he is full of sound and fury.

THROUGH GREAT TRIBULATION

Though victory is the future of God's people, the road to new creation is marked by trials in this world. Jesus said, "In the world you will have tribulation" (John 16:33). Paul taught that through many tribulations we must enter the kingdom (Acts 14:22). These troubles are light and momentary when compared to the coming glory that awaits us (2 Cor. 4:17). The book of Revelation teaches this too, which is why endurance is among its major themes.

From the world's perspective, the suffering of Christians might seem like defeat. But what if worldly loss leads to eternal gain? What if temporary sufferings give way to unending blessings? Jesus promised, "The one who conquers, I will grant him to sit with me on my throne, as I also conquered and sat down with my Father on his throne" (Rev. 3:21).

Persevering in suffering for Christ *is* conquering. And Revelation 7 describes a multitude of conquerors: "After this I looked, and behold, a great multitude that no one could number, from every nation, from all tribes and peoples and languages, standing before the throne and before the Lamb, clothed in white robes" (Rev. 7:9). A heavenly elder told John, "These are the ones coming out of the great tribulation. They have washed their robes and made them white in the blood of the Lamb" (7:14).

Believers from John's generation faced suffering. In subsequent centuries, too, Christians have suffered in the face of hostility from the serpent and the principalities of this world. The readers of Revelation should not be surprised, then, by the antagonism of the wicked. John's visions prepare us for suffering, encouraging us to be faithful unto death so as to receive the crown of life. Throughout church history, millions of Christians have been martyred, but because they belonged to Christ, their death was gain (Phil. 1:21).

Tribulation is followed by vindication, and this hope is why the saints of Christ will endure affliction. A heavenly voice said, "Blessed are the dead who die in the Lord from now on," and the Spirit said, "Blessed indeed, that they may rest from their labors, for their deeds follow them!" (Rev. 14:13). The blessing for the faithful is the fulfillment of Jesus' words in Matthew 5:10–12: "Blessed are those who are persecuted for righteousness' sake, for theirs is the kingdom of heaven. Blessed are you when others revile you and persecute you and utter all kinds of evil against you falsely on my account. Rejoice and be glad, for your reward is great in heaven, for so they persecuted the prophets who were before you."

The book of Revelation confirms the promise of Jesus: the reward for the persecuted is great. Theirs is the kingdom of heaven.

THE DEFEAT OF DEATH

Flesh and blood cannot inherit the kingdom of God—mortal flesh and blood, that is. God will raise his people to receive all that he has promised and prepared for them. Since the perishable cannot inherit the imperishable, the perishable must put on what is imperishable (1 Cor. 15:50). The saints must be raised from the dead to everlasting bodily life and glory.

The New Testament documents are brimming with the hope of death's defeat. The Gospels, Acts, Letters, and Apocalypse all hold forth this hope. In Revelation 20, the description is of death's defeat at Christ's return:

> *And I saw the dead, great and small, standing before the throne, and books were opened. Then another book was opened, which is the book of life. And the dead were judged by what was written in the books, according to what they had done. And the sea gave up the dead who were in it, Death and Hades gave up the dead who were in them, and they were judged, each one of them, according to what they had done (Rev. 20:12–13).*

The scene in Revelation 20:12–13 is parallel to Jesus' words in Matthew 25:

> *When the Son of Man comes in his glory, and all the angels with him, then he will sit on his glorious throne. Before him will be gathered*

> *all the nations, and he will separate people one from another as a shepherd separates the sheep from the goats. And he will place the sheep on his right, but the goats on the left (Matt. 25:31–33).*

Being "gathered" to appear before the Son of Man is a bodily gathering through resurrection. This is the gathering Paul refers to: "For we must all appear before the judgment seat of Christ, so that each one may receive what is due for what he has done in the body, whether good or evil" (2 Cor. 5:10).

Those who suffer bodily have the hope of bodily resurrection because Christ himself has authority over death. He said, "Fear not, I am the first and the last, and the living one. I died, and behold I am alive forevermore, and I have the keys of Death and Hades" (Rev. 1:17–18). Jesus is the resurrection and the life (John 11:25), and he will prove that claim for all his people. They will be raised immortal.

Believers are not the only ones who will be raised. The general resurrection will encompass unbelievers as well, but they will not be raised to bodily glory. They will be raised for condemnation. Jesus spoke of the unrighteous rising with the righteous (Matt. 12:41–42). Paul referred to the resurrection of the just and the unjust (Acts 24:15). According to Revelation 20, "if anyone's name was not found written in the book of life, he was thrown into the lake of fire" (Rev. 20:15).

The wicked will be raised to face the second death.

FINAL JUDGMENT

The Old and New Testament authors speak with one voice that the wicked will face the judgment of the holy and righteous God. This is the ultimate Day of the Lord, the day of wrath, the day when the wicked reap what they have sown. God's perfect justice should fill the wicked with dread and prompt their repentance. His perfect justice should fill the righteous with joy and prompt their praise.

The book of Psalms sings about the downfall of the wicked. Surrounded by enemies, the psalmists cry out for deliverance and celebrate the collapse of conspiracies and assaults. David said, "In just a little while, the wicked will be no more; though you look carefully at his place, he will not be there" (Ps. 37:10). Elsewhere he prayed, "Pour out your indignation upon them, and let your burning anger overtake them" (Ps. 69:24).

No matter what earthly consequences and griefs the wicked face because of their sins, no temporary judgment was the final judgment. The wicked die in the first death, the physical death that comes upon all people in a fallen world. But the wicked will face something the righteous will not: "the second death" (Rev. 20:6, 14; 21:8). The second death is the unending condemnation of the wicked.

When John reports the response of the saints to the judgment of the wicked in Revelation 19, the saints rejoice: "Hallelujah! Salvation and glory and power belong to our God, for his judgments are true and just; for he has judged the great prostitute who corrupted the earth with her immorality, and has avenged on her the blood of his servants" (Rev. 19:1–2). The singers are celebrating the righteous vengeance of God, for he has done what is true and just.

The final judgment will be beyond reproach, for God is holy. His goodness and wisdom cannot be compromised by bribes, manipulation, deception, neglect, or oversight. While earthly judicial systems are susceptible to corruption by sinners, divine justice is not so.

Not only will the wicked face the perfect righteousness of God at the final judgment, but the devil and his demons will be eternally condemned as well. Jesus spoke of hell as "prepared for the devil and his angels" (Matt. 25:41). And the wicked will go there as well, into eternal punishment (25:46). Revelation 20:10 says the devil "was thrown into the lake of fire and sulfur." The devil will not reign as a prince of hell. He will be cast down, overcome, and condemned.

While the final judgment of the wicked is an important biblical doctrine, it is not the last of Revelation's visions. John has more to say because there was more to see. And what he saw was a new creation.

ALL THINGS NEW

The New Testament ends where the beginning of the Old Testament was pointing all along. At the beginning of Genesis, we read that God created the heavens and the earth (Gen. 1:1). And at the end of Revelation, we read that

John saw a new heaven and a new earth (Rev. 21:1).

Since the corruption of sin and death pervaded not just God's image-bearers but all creation as well, the redemptive work of God will bring newness to all creation. Revelation 21–22 narrate the liberation of the heavens and the earth from the bondage of decay and futility (Rom. 8:19–23). The effects of sin—like mourning and pain and death—will pass away (Rev. 21:4).

The one who said, "Let there be light" (Gen. 1:3) will say, "Behold, I am making all things new" (Rev. 21:5). And things shall be as he says. Every good and bright thing in this life is but a glimpse, a taste, of what God shall do in and for his people throughout everlasting days. No frailties shall burden us. No worries shall preoccupy us. No afflictions shall grieve us. No tears shall empty us. No sin shall tempt us.

Forever united to Christ, we will know a kind of life that cannot end. We shall reign with him. The kingdom's inauguration will reach its consummation, its fullness. In this fullness we will live, move, and have our being. We will be exiles no more.

We will be home.

UNDERSTANDING JESUS

- The reality of Christ's reign and his authority over death should encourage the perseverance of the saints.
- Though the devil opposes Christ and persecutes the people of Christ, the devil's time is short as history heads toward the day of his judgment.
- The return of Christ will bring about the resurrection of the righteous and the wicked, and the subsequent judgment will establish eternal states for both.
- The new creation will be the eternal home for Christ and his people, where they shall dwell in the light and peace and joy and glory of God.

SUGGESTED READING

- Psalm 16
- Isaiah 25
- Romans 8:18–30
- 1 Thessalonians 4:13 – 5:11

RECOMMENDED RESOURCES

For further reading on the kinds of things that the previous chapters addressed in this book, I recommend these resources for your instruction and enjoyment.

Paul Barnett, *The Birth of Christianity: The First Twenty Years*, After Jesus, vol. 1 (Grand Rapids: William B. Eerdmans, 2005).

Paul Barnett, *Paul: Missionary of Jesus*, After Jesus, vol. 2 (Grand Rapids: William B. Eerdmans, 2008).

G. K. Beale and Benjamin Gladd, *The Story Retold: A Biblical-Theological Introduction to the New Testament* (Grand Rapids: IVP Academic, 2020).

Mitchell Chase, *Hope for All the Earth: Understanding the Story of the Old Testament* (Leyland: 10Publishing, 2022).

Mitchell Chase, *Resurrection Hope and the Death of Death,* Short Studies in Biblical Theology (Wheaton: Crossway, 2022).

Brandon Crowe, *The Message of the General Epistles in the History of Redemption: Wisdom from James, Peter, John, and Jude* (Phillipsburg: P&R, 2015).

Andreas Köstenberger and Alexander Stewart, *The First Days of Jesus: The Story of the Incarnation* (Wheaton: Crossway, 2015).

Andreas Köstenberger and Justin Taylor, *The Final Days of Jesus: The Most Important Week of the Most Important Person Who Ever Lived* (Wheaton: Crossway, 2014).

Patrick Schreiner, *The Ascension of Christ: Recovering a Neglected Doctrine* (Bellingham: Lexham Press, 2020).

Patrick Schreiner, *The Mission of the Triune God: A Theology of Acts*, New Testament Theology (Wheaton: Crossway, 2022).

Thomas Schreiner, *The Joy of Hearing: A Theology of the Book of Revelation*, New Testament Theology (Wheaton: Crossway, 2021).

Thomas Schreiner, *Paul, Apostle of God's Glory in Christ: A Pauline Theology*, 2nd ed. (Grand Rapids: IVP Academic, 2020).

More books from 10Publishing

Resources that point to Jesus

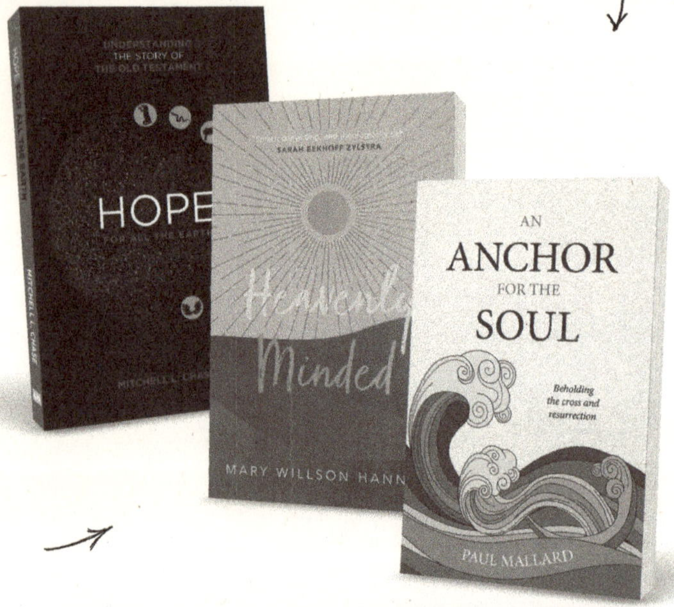